Region-Building in West Africa

This book examines the role of the Economic Community of West African States (ECOWAS) practitioners in coordinating, creating, and managing regional governance practices in the areas of public health, peace and security, and microfinancial integration.

Since 1975, there have been many failed and successful attempts at unconstitutional government changes in West Africa. During this same period, numerous instruments have been designed to promote peace and security in the region. This book examines the role of bureaucratic actors in the ECOWAS in harmonizing regional integration policy in West Africa. Using data from fieldwork in several countries in West Africa, Balogun observes how ECOWAS practitioners network and strategically engage regional stakeholders in health, peace and security, and finance as a means to deepen harmonization between ECOWAS Member States and build a connection with civil society. Balogun argues that the founding conditions of ECOWAS set the organization on an institutional path to adapt its approaches to regional governance.

Region-building in West Africa challenges the idea that self-interested leaders limit regional cooperation. The book also challenges the idea that the bureaucrats in the organization are glorified servants to their governments. Region-building in West Africa instead focuses on the influence that bureaucrats have in shaping the international policy agenda of ECOWAS.

This book will be useful to scholars, students, and practitioners in Africa and beyond who want to better understand the inner workings of African regional organizations, and the processes that drive cooperation across West Africa.

Emmanuel Balogun is Assistant Professor of Political Science and affiliate faculty in Black Studies at Skidmore College.

New Regionalisms Series
Series Editor: Timothy M. Shaw

The *New Regionalisms* series presents innovative analyses of a range of novel regional relations & institutions. Going beyond formal, interstate organisations, this interdisciplinary Series builds on over two decades of the pioneering International Political Economy of New Regionalisms series, also edited by Professor Timothy M. Shaw.

New Regionalisms is creative & cosmopolitan, reflecting enquiries from & about the global South & North. It reinforces ongoing networks of analysts in both academia & think-tanks as well as international institutions concerned with micro-, meso- & macro-level regionalisms in the third decade of the 21st century & beyond.

For more information about this series, please visit: www.routledge.com/New-Regionalisms-Series/book-series/ASHSER1146

Mapping Arctic Paradiplomacy
Limits and Opportunities for Sub-National Actors in Arctic Governance
Edited by Mathieu Landriault, Jean-François Payette and Stéphane Roussel

China-EU Relations in a New Era of Global Transformation
Edited by Li Xing

Weak States, Vulnerable Governments, and Regional Cooperation
An ASEAN Case Study
Ştefania Atena Feraru

Constructing the East African Community
Diffusion from African and European Regional Organizations
Mariel Reiss

Region-Building in West Africa
Convergence and Agency in ECOWAS
Emmanuel Balogun

Disruptions and Rhetoric in African Development Policy
George Kararach

Region-Building in West Africa

Convergence and Agency in ECOWAS

Emmanuel Balogun

Routledge
Taylor & Francis Group
LONDON AND NEW YORK

First published 2022
by Routledge
4 Park Square, Milton Park, Abingdon, Oxon OX14 4RN

and by Routledge
605 Third Avenue, New York, NY 10158

Routledge is an imprint of the Taylor & Francis Group, an informa business

British Library Cataloguing-in-Publication Data
A catalogue record for this book is available from the British Library

Library of Congress Cataloging-in-Publication Data
A catalog record has been requested for this book

ISBN: 978-1-138-34832-5 (hbk)
ISBN: 978-1-032-22748-1 (pbk)
ISBN: 978-0-429-43673-4 (ebk)

DOI: 10.4324/9780429436734

Typeset in Times New Roman
by Newgen Publishing UK

Dedicated to Lauren, Violet, and Amina.

Contents

About the Author

Emmanuel Balogun is an assistant professor of Political Science and affiliate faculty in Black Studies at Skidmore College. He is a 2021–2022 Council on Foreign Relations International Affairs Fellow and the inaugural Diversity Fellow at the Bridging the Gap Project. His research focuses on African regional organizations, global health governance, and peace and security governance. He is the recipient of a Fulbright-Hays Group Project Abroad Grant to study Pan-Africanism in Ghana, and his research is featured, published, and forthcoming in *International Affairs*, *African Studies Review*, *Africa Spectrum*, *Oxford Research Encyclopedia of International Studies, the Washington Post*, *BBC, and Oxford Analytica.* He earned his PhD and MA at the University of Delaware, MA from Western Illinois University, and BA from New England College.

Acknowledgments

I owe an immense amount of gratitude to a lot of people who have been so supportive and inspiring to me throughout the process of writing this book. I will never be able to thank these people in the way that they deserve, but in writing these acknowledgments, I am reminded how incredibly lucky and blessed I am to have these individuals in my life. I am so grateful to my amazing mentors, Alice Ba, Gretchen Bauer, and David C. Wilson. Thank you all so much for your guidance and support through all the phases of writing and career moves that precede the publication of this book. I would also like to thank Claire Maloney and Robert Sorsby for their generosity and grace. I would not have the opportunity to write this book if it were not for Professor Timothy Shaw. Thank you for your incredible patience and unwavering support. It is an honor to be one of the many in your intellectual family tree.

Of course, the book would not be possible without the gracious and generous colleagues at the ECOWAS Commission, particularly Steve Onuwuka, the entire Political and Peace and Security Commission, Hyacenth Okwu, Alozie Amaechi Godfrey, Michel Saraka, Dr. Babatunde Idowu, and Jerome Boa among many others. I am also indebted to the entire staff at the ECOWAS Library and Archives. Thanks to the collaborators at WAHO, particularly Dr. Kofi Busia, Dr. Issiaka Sombie, Harvey De Kadt, Bernard Thierry, and Annick Sidbe. Immense gratitude to Nana Afadzinu, Chukwuemeka Eze, Franklin Oduro, and Allimou Diallo.

I am grateful for the support of the Skidmore College Department of Political Science, particularly my chair, Natalie Taylor, Beau Breslin, Kate Graney, Yelena Bieberman-Ockali, Feryaz Ocakli, Bob Turner, Flagg Taylor, Christopher Mann, Ron Seyb, and Barbara McDonough. Thank you all so much. I am also so grateful to the Bridging the Gap team, particularly Naazneen Barma, Brent Durbin, Jordan Tama, James Goldgeier, Bruce Jentleson, Dani Gilbert, Erik Lin-Greenberg, Rachel Whitlark, Leila Adler, Kathryn Urban, and Sara Plana. I am also grateful to my student research assistants, Fatima Isa, Jasmindar Singh, Lexie Salamone, Anissa Joseph, Serita Lewis, and Sumitra Dhakal.

They say "steel sharpens steel," and I have been so inspired by the current crop of great scholars of African regionalism. Thank you to Thomas Tieku,

Cyril Obi, Lembe Tiky, Densua Mumford, Lynda Iroulo, Kwesi Aning, Okey Iheduru, Nicole de Silva, Jens Herpolsheimer, Anna Mwaba, Folashadé Soulé-Kohndou, Amanda Coffie, J. Andrew Grant, and Edward Akuffo.

I have also benefitted from the advice and support of some brilliant collaborators outside of the realm of African regionalism. Thanks to my friends and co-authors Aarie Glas, Amy Patterson, John Ishiyama, and Joseph Oppong. I could not have gone through the process of writing without great friends and mentors who always hold me accountable: Kim Yi Dionne, Pinar Alakoc, Faith Okpotor, Chiedo Nwankwor, Rachel Cantave, S. Donny Bellamy, Mary Kate Donovan, Samantha Kelley, Molly Ariotti, Terri Givens, Steve Nkurlu, Elsa Fan, Shazia Ahmed, and Yolande Bouka. Thank you all so much for being there for me in more ways than you know.

I could not do this without my family. It was my father Kazeem who inspired me to return home and learn more about West Africa. My mother Rita, who made sure I was taking care of myself throughout the process. To my parents and biggest supporters Mary-Ellen and Vincent Hylton. My sisters Shanaye, Elizabeth, and Trish; brother Abraham, thank you for all you do. Finally, I want to thank my wife Lauren and my incredible daughters, Violet and Amina. You all have made my life full of meaning and purpose. I love you all so much and thank you for making my life so special.

Abbreviations

AAFC	Allied Armed Forces of the Community
AEC	African Economic Community
AEF	Afrique équatoriale Française
AfCFTA	African Continental Free Trade Agreement
AFRO	World Health Organization's Regional Office for Africa
ALG	Authorite du liptako gourma/liptako gourma authority
AOF	Afrique occidentale Française
ASEAN	Association of Southeast Asian Nations
ATS	Amphetamine Type Stimulants
AU	African Union
AUDA	African Union Development Agency
BCEAO	Banque Centrale des Etats de l'Afrique de l'Ouest/Central Bank of West African States
BI	Bamako Initiative
BIAWE	Business Incubator for African Women Entrepreneurs
BVRM	Bourse Régionale des Valeurs Mobiliéres
CDD	the Center of Democracy and Development
CEAO	Economic Community of West African States (Communauté économique des États de l'Afrique de l'Ouest)
CEMLAWS	Centre for Maritime laws Africa
CET	Common External Tarrif
CFA	Communatué financière d'Afrique/African Financial Community
CIDA	Canadian International Development Agency
CILSS	Permanent Interstate Committee for drought control in the Sahel
CORDS	Connecting Organizations for Regional Disease Surveillance
COVID	Coronavirus Disease
CSO	Civil Society Organization
D.C	District of Columbia
EAC	East African Community
EAIDSnet	East African Integrated Disease Network
EBID	ECOWAS Bank of Investment and Development

ECA	United Nations Economic Commission for Africa
ECCAS	Economic Community of Central African States
ECOMIG	ECOWAS Mission to The Gambia
ECOMOG	Economic Community of West African States Monitoring Group
ECOWARN	ECOWAS Early Warning and Response Network
ECOWAS	Economic Community of West African States
ECPF	ECOWAS Conflict Prevention Framework
EERT	ECOWAS Emergency Response Team
EIMS	ECOWAS Integrated Maritime Strategy
EPA	Economic Partnership Agreement
ESF	ECOWAS Standby Force
EU	European Union
FAO	Food and Agriculture Organization
FDI	Foreign Direct Investment
GDP	Gross Domestic Product
GGC	Gulf of Guinea Commission
GIABA	Inter-Governmental Action Group against Money Laundering in West Africa
HIV/AIDS	Human Immunodeficiency Virus/Acquired Immunodeficiency Syndrome
HME	Hierarchical Market Economies
IBTC	Investment Banking and Trust Company
IDP	Internally Displaced Person
ILO	International Labor Organization
IMF	International Monetary Fund
INN	International Negotiation Network
KAIPTC	Kofi Annan International Peacekeeping Training Centre
MFI	Microfinance Institutions
MNC	Multinational Corporations
MoU	Memorandum of Understanding
MRU	Mano River Union
MSF	Medicines Sans Frontiers/Doctors Without Borders
NCD	Non-Communicable Disease
NEPAD	New Partnership for Africa's Development
NGO	Non-governmental Organizations
NPC	National Peace Council
NPFL	National Patriotic Front of Liberia
OAU	Organisation of African Unity
OCAM	Organization Commune Africaine et Malgache/African and Malagasy Union
OCCGE	Organisation de coordination pour la lute contre le grandes endemes
OERS	Organization of the Senegal River States
PAPS	Political Affairs, Peace and Security commission

PSC	Peace and Security Council
RCSDC	Regional Centre for Surveillance and Disease Control
RCSO	Regional Civil Society Organizations
REC	Regional Economic Communities
REWARD	Reacting to Early Warning and Response Data
RIP	Regional Indicative Programme
SACIDS	South African Centre for Infectious Disease and Surveillance
SADC	Southern African Development Community
SMC	Standing Mediation Committee
UEMOA	Union Economique et Monetaire Ouest Africain/Economic and Monetary Union of West Africa
UN	United Nations
UNAIDS	United Nations Programme on HIV/AIDS
UNCDF	United Nations Capital Development Funds
UNDP	United Nations Development Programme
UNICEF	United Nations International Children's Emergency Funds
UNODC	United Nations office for Drugs and Crime
USAID	United States Agency for International Development
WACD	West Africa Commission on Drugs
WACSI	West African Civil Society Institute
WACSOF	West African Civil Society Forum
WAEMU	West African Economic and Monetary Union
WAHC	West African Health Community
WAHO	West African Health Organization
WAMA	West African Monetary Association
WANEP	West African Networking for Peacebuilding
WANIDS	West African Network for Infectious Disease Surveillance
WHO	World Health Organization

1 Introduction

In early August 2019, over 100 staff members at the Economic Community of West African States (ECOWAS) Commission in Abuja, Nigeria, gathered and held a candlelight vigil to recognize the life of a fellow staff member who died suddenly in the previous week. Typically, the ECOWAS Commission is a fast-moving place, filled with international diplomats, career civil servants, and consultants, and the occasional West African politicians speaking a multitude of languages—from Twi, Wolof, Yoruba, Igbo, French, Portuguese, and English—maneuver around the building with haste. However, in this moment, everyone in the building stood still, praying and embracing each other, as they remembered their colleague's energy, spirit, and contribution to ECOWAS.

The show of support and the words spoken about the recently departed staff member paint a picture of what the ECOWAS Commission purports to stand for: diversity of people, ideas, positions, and mandates within the daily operation of the organization, uniquely one, and tied to each other by a shared vision. The speakers at the vigil intimated as much, calling for those in attendance to remember to "take care of each other" and that "they need each other to make [ECOWAS] work." Despite the somberness of the vigil, there was a connectedness of a group of people who viewed their relationships with each other as the key to being effective in their jobs. The vigil also paints a different picture of an organization in ECOWAS, which has been considered to be insular and elite, motivated not by unity in diversity, but by unity in the desire to preserve power among self-interested West African leaders.[1]

ECOWAS has long posed a puzzle of the study of regionalism and international relations. Created on May 28, 1975 through the Treaty of Lagos, ECOWAS consists of member states diverse in political and economic capacity, having differing experiences with colonialism, and having competing interests from actors external to the region. The region has been slow in its path toward economic integration, particularly the establishment of a common currency. Profound economic and material inequalities exist between member states, which contribute to the hurdles of integration. Politically, member states have varying experiences with democracy and good governance, evidenced by the legacy of military rule, regional heads of states' attempts to pursue unconstitutional government changes, and civil conflicts.

DOI: 10.4324/9780429436734-1

Other theoretical perspectives such as neofunctionalism and neoliberal institutionalism, explain ECOWAS' experience with regional integration as a failure to embrace and respond to market-based approaches to regional organization. A lack of intra-West African trade, insignificant trade diversion, high trading costs, and the lack of implementation of trade liberalization schemes are often cited as reasons why regional integration has largely failed.[2] Alongside the trade and development obstacles, West Africa has had a turbulent experience with democracy. Despite the fact that in 2017, for the first time since the creation of ECOWAS, all of its heads of states have been at least nominally elected into power, there has been a significant number of coup attempts and attempts by various heads of states over the last 44 years to change their constitutions to remain in power.[3]

While the original intent of ECOWAS was to facilitate economic integration, the organization evolved to enhance its role in facilitating political and peace and security cooperation in West Africa. ECOWAS expanded its mandate into social and welfare governance. This allowed ECOWAS to include civilian actors and non-state stakeholders into the governance process. This process, which ECOWAS terms as a "transformation from an ECOWAS of States to an ECOWAS of people" is puzzling given how approaches to regional integration attribute ECOWAS' survival to the desire of self-interested heads of states who want to raise their formal status and maintain existing regimes, rather than serve public interests.[4] Regional cooperation, under this notion, occurs because African states are inherently weak and lack transparency and a way to manage the limited development capacities of West African states.[5]

However, the regional dynamics in West Africa tells a different story. The ECOWAS Vision 2020 document, created during the ECOWAS' 40th anniversary, created a new comprehensive harmonization strategy defined by the "unifying tenets of a West African shared vision." These tenets call each member state to develop region-centric national development policies managed by specific stakeholders within ECOWAS and national civil society actors. ECOWAS Vision 2020 also states all member states to "demonstrably have undertaken the required constitutional and administrative measures to entrench regional approaches and create national implementing agencies needed to implement ECOWAS programs" to ensure proper regional oversight jurisprudence in implementing customs and common market institutions.

On a continental level, the legacy of Pan-Africanism underscores the creation and recreation of regional unity and integration. Kwame Nkrumah, first president of Ghana after independence, often made the argument that there were differences in the approach to integration and that African nations had a shared, common destiny to develop their own economic integration and combat neocolonialism of the European market. The common destiny argument served as the primary rallying cry of Pan-Africanist proponents of the Organization of African Unity (OAU). Currently, the African Union (AU) resuscitates and reinvents Pan-Africanism by creating a universal African identity through the linking of diverse and complex social networks and relations.[6] The resurgence of the AU and its positioning as a supranational entity place regional organizations such as ECOWAS as subsidiaries, engulfed into a larger form of cooperation. While the AU has been progressive in developing a coherent strategy toward unifying Africa, regional economic communities (or RECs) have been slow to fully integrate into the larger continental organization, and instead, leading RECs to operate within their subregional frameworks. Further, issues of subsidiarity and paternalism with the United Nations (UN) shortchange the role of subregional organizations and relegate them to the service of larger regional or international organizations.[7] Increased attention on the AU and its role in responding to unconstitutional changes in government and peace and security governance across Africa also brings to question the relevance of organizations such as ECOWAS and its contributions to international peace and security norms.

How does ECOWAS arrive at this notion of an "ECOWAS of people?" What explains the institutional trajectory of ECOWAS? How can we reconcile ECOWAS' institutional innovation with the claim that the organization only serves at the privilege of its heads of states?

While the success of market and currency integration in ECOWAS has been mixed at best, the processes of institutional change have led to the emergence of a community of practice that creates values around democracy and good governance and emphasizes the development of a more inclusive mode of governance that places civilian capacity to manage governance over the self-interest of heads of states of Government. In understanding the processes of ECOWAS' institutional development and change, we gain insight into the construction of West Africa's "region-ness" and how it diverges from conventional regionalization approaches.[8]

Region-building in West Africa is concerned with examining how ECOWAS mediates the institution's interests while simultaneously using the organization to bring disparate regional actors together to manage regional governance. A conception of region-building that emphasizes people-centrism and the integration of multiple regional stakeholders into regional governance offers another way to assess regionalism in Africa differently than perspectives that emphasize dynamics of regime boosting and self-interest by political leaders (Grant and Fredrik 2003). Instead, this account examines how the process of convergence is made to be inclusive to actors across scales of governance and how said inclusivity enhances actor agency. This account of region-building and regional convergence explores how ECOWAS from its inception to its current iteration engages in a convergence process to develop regional identity and community by engaging in practices that bring in multiple regional stakeholders into the regional governance space. Practices are competent, socially meaningful performances that generate patterns of interaction.[9] These practices contribute to a process of institutional change in

ECOWAS—meaning changes in the structure of the organization and changing the entrenchment of rules and norms within ECOWAS.

Who is responsible for implementing and interpreting these new rules and norms? In the process of region-building in ECOWAS, the international bureaucrats or the practitioners/officials constituted within ECOWAS serve as the "connective tissue" of regional governance. They are responsible for creating the institutional documents that represent the rules and norms of the organization. They are responsible for interpreting the mandate of the organization as dictated by the Authority heads of state. They are the key actors who engage and liaise with civil society actors, not just regime leaders. Focusing on the makeup of ECOWAS practitioners and the activities of ECOWAS practitioners allows for an inquiry into how those responsible for the everyday functioning of ECOWAS are able to acquire and use their autonomy to engage in policy initiation and evaluation. By looking at the activities of ECOWAS practitioners, we are able to decipher what practices are important for region-building and understand the process of how the said practices become critical to the institutional structure of ECOWAS.

Thus, *Region-Building in West Africa* examines ECOWAS in a way that focuses on *practices and agency* as a pathway to understand how bureaucrats in a seemingly insular and elite-led regional organization can exert influence and create a more inclusive regional governance. By focusing on practices and agency as conduits of region-building, this book uncovers both the self-evident and discrete dynamics of the relationship between agency and institutional change.

Regional Cooperation in West Africa

Who are the drivers of regional cooperation in West Africa? Are these drivers responsible for the content, substance, and form of cooperation in region configurations in Africa? How do these drivers shape the complexion of ECOWAS? To whom are the drivers of regional cooperation accountable, and how do the drivers of regional cooperation in West Africa develop or obtain the capacity to engage stakeholders in regional cooperation processes?

Answers to these questions require examining the distribution of power, inclination toward cooperation, and the ability for actors to shape the course of cooperation superseding competing interests by multiple parties. One definition of regionalism privileges the multifaceted and comprehensive role of the state and non-state actors as well as a range of political, economic, strategic, social, demographic, and ecological interactions within regions.[10] New Regionalism approaches shift the focus away from formal institutions toward studying informal sectors, parallel economies, and non-state coalitions. Regionalism is also an analytic response to uneven globalizations, the proliferation of states, and the rise of non-state actors (particularly private companies and civil societies).[11] These approaches to understanding regionalism suggest that the management, structure, and processes of regional governance occurs in different spheres of authority, and within those spheres, a multiplicity of actors can develop the capacity to shape processes of regional cooperation.

However, what has typically distinguished regionalism and regional cooperation in West Africa is the characterization of the African state. Seen as traditionally weak, the structure and leadership of West African states subjects the emergence and development of regionalism to state power asymmetries in facilitating regionalization processes (Herbst 2000; Villalón 2005). Regionalism, according to this perspective, becomes a venue for states to project images, garner prestige, and alleviate notions that their state or regional processes are not devoid of adherence to global norms and best practices of regional integration. Tethering regionalism in West Africa solely to the realpolitik, reaffirmation, and political will/competition of head of states limits the full scope of actors that shape and drive cooperation beyond the heads of states of government. Thus, it is important to reorient the analysis of regionalism in West Africa to highlight the specific issue areas and the context in which regional cooperation occurs in West Africa, to understand how multiple actors within the West African sphere of authority emerge and manage governance, to identifying the mechanisms that drive cooperation, and toward understanding the mutual constitution of formal structures and informal networks, as well as possible emergent or alternative perspectives of regionalism.

Reorienting or redefining the distinctiveness of regionalism in West Africa accounts for and incorporates the diversity among actors. Rather than emphasizing the ways in which differences among actors delimit possibilities for regional cooperation, a redefinition of regionalism in West Africa considers regionalism as "the pursuit of regional unity as a response to the understood problems of division."[12] Emphasizing how differences bring actors together stresses the importance of the processes that lead to shared understandings of how delicately states within the region relate to each other. For instance, in an example outside of Africa, the Association of Southeast Asian Nations (ASEAN) "[are] morally-bound-not to push regionalism too hard or too far lest the whole project fall apart," making regional unity a driver and constraint to ASEAN regionalism.[13] Thus, a redefinition of regionalism in the West African context is one that not only accounts for the multiplicity of actors but also accounts for the diversity among said actors and how, when put together, these actors develop a more coherent perspective of regionalism and drive region-building.

A redefinition of regionalism that understands considers unity in diversity also requires a reconsideration of which actors we privilege. A redefinition of regionalism in West Africa emphasizes how regionalism and its associated processes should consider specific regional activities and processes of inclusion of other actors such as the bureaucratic practitioners within a regional organization and others that engage in policy evaluation and formation.[14] Put differently, reorienting regional cooperation in West Africa to focus on the bureaucratic practitioners moves beyond the singular focus of the behaviors and interests of West African heads of states and toward the activities of the practitioners that constitute the everyday operations of regional governance—the actual "managers" of regional governance.

By focusing on how bureaucratic practitioners unite the region despite the diversity of regional actors, we can understand how their ideas about regional cooperation diffuse throughout the region. A focus on practitioner-led regionalism links scales from the regional to the global, focusing on activities that operate in between macro-level forces and every day human interactions. Rather than emphasizing the quality of West African statehood or the constraints posed by West African heads of state and their self-interests, a practitioner-led approach to regional governance points to the emergence and importance of new actors and the agency they possess to shape and develop norms and ideas around regional governance.

This book challenges the prevalent view that heads of state in West Africa and Africa more broadly use regional organizations to engage and sustain clientelism and neopatrimonialism in an effort to preserve their narrow self-interests. Instead, this book amends the proclivity to tether the region's construction to the assumptions of the logic of neopatrimonialism as applied to African states by focusing on the activities, practices, and strategies practitioners use to implement institutional change.

This book argues that ECOWAS practitioners can acquire agency due to two institutional features: organizational dynamism and bureaucratic autonomy. Organizational dynamism refers to ECOWAS' tendency to change the institutional rules and norms of the organization in response to crises or external pressure from other actors in the region. Bureaucratic autonomy refers to the institutional space given to officials to engage in and conduct regional governance, meaning that ECOWAS practitioners are not directly subject to direct oversight and management by the organization's core decision-making entity.

Why ECOWAS?

Of all the RECs in Africa, ECOWAS has one of the more developed institutional frameworks of regional governance. The revision of its founding treaty in 1993 and subsequent protocols expanded the scope of ECOWAS' activities to include peace and security, the establishment and maintenance of democracy and good governance, and social policy. While there may be a tendency to view the expanded mandate as mission creep, these new values have led to a convergence of values that permeate throughout West Africa, even in the context of external actors and conflicting motivations by member states. Therefore, ECOWAS serves as a fruitful case study to understand the extent to which ideas of regional convergence and region-building cultivate regional identity, while also examining how regional identity formation and institutional change contribute to the durability of ECOWAS.

ECOWAS, founded in 1975, has transformed its existence, governance structures, and its shared values. ECOWAS has undergone two transformations. First, it existed primarily as an organization focused on economic integration, but it revised their treaty in 1993 to become more of a political union, and later transformed their governance structure to a commission in 2006. Central to identifying the role of convergence and agency is understanding social context in which practitioners engage with each other and with other regional stakeholders—and how said social context influences ECOWAS' institutions. For example, when understanding the context in which practitioners develop and engage with ECOWAS' peace and security mandate, we can better understand institutional developments and evolution around peace and security. Similarly, understanding the diversity of actors and competing interests between Anglophone West African States and their Francophone counterparts allows one to decipher the tensions around adopting a common West African currency and the potential hurdles of integrating the continental trade regime, the African Continental Free Trade Area (AfCFTA). ECOWAS' response to the enduring coronavirus disease-2019 (COVID-19) pandemic also highlights the significance of understanding how practitioners work to create a harmonized, regional response, despite the significant variation in how each member state is responding. The focal point of this book is to highlight the manner in which convergence occurs and the capacity for practitioners within ECOWAS to facilitate convergence. Assuming that convergence is a central feature of regional organization, this book questions and analyzes how convergence happens.

ECOWAS Practitioners and Communities of Practice

ECOWAS practitioners can be considered a community of practice. Communities of practice consist of actors who derive their patterns of interaction from a shared background knowledge that includes inherent discussions as to what is permissible and appropriate within a group of actors.[15] In ECOWAS, practitioners share common and institutionalized means of cooperation, bounded not only by the physical space of the ECOWAS Commission but also by the institutional rules of ECOWAS. Thus, practitioners within the ECOWAS community of practice not only work within the ECOWAS Commission in Abuja but also operate in other institutional spaces such as workshop and trainings, ministerial meetings, summits, and more. The ECOWAS commission and these other hubs are places where norms are adopted and created by practitioners and serve as the source of background knowledge for practitioners.

ECOWAS practitioners are typically not considered to be political appointees from member state governments. Meaning, that though practitioners may come from individual member states, their mandate is not to represent the interests of their country; rather, they are independent actors within the organization there to do work in the best interest of the organization. In simple terms, they are considered to be regional civil servants, with the task of serving the regional community.

ECOWAS practitioners come to the organization via procurement calls and recruitment. Some practitioners have held posts in their member state governments, most have held posts at other international organizations. ECOWAS practitioners are considered career professionals and international bureaucrats. ECOWAS practitioners exist to satisfy the collective needs of the organization. As one practitioner noted in one of our first meetings, "ECOWAS is primarily about the states, and that is our job first, but we also have our own jobs [to do]."[16] Based on their prior experiences in other bureaucratic contexts, ECOWAS practitioners mirror their other international civil servant counterparts and possess technical expertise and bureaucratic skill that inform their capacity to shape the institution. In this vein, ECOWAS practitioners serve as "engines of integration" rather than "obedient servants" to member states, as they are able to rely on their independence, autonomy, and expertise to influence governance outcomes.[17] Xu and Weller in their study of international civil servants argue that in order to explain how international organizations and states are affected by international civil servants, we must consider informal factors such as competence, ability, legitimacy, culture, and institutional opportunity structures to see how international civil servants develop the capacity to affect the organization. Considering how ECOWAS practitioners are imbued with these factors, this book contributes to the study of international civil servants and their roles as bureaucratic actors by examining the means by which the competence, technical expertise, ability, and culture of international civil servants are informed by and inform the institutional structure of ECOWAS and its governance outputs. As such, it is important to understand the specific mechanisms that make ECOWAS practitioners central to regional governance.

Practices are a useful framework to examine the context in which ECOWAS practitioners operate from shared background knowledge, which informs their capacity to act within the autonomous bureaucratic structure of the ECOWAS Commission. As noted by Adler and Pouliot in their work on International Practices, any given practice can be appraised through different levels of aggregation. They use the example of international summitry as an example of one aggregate practice or, if one zooms in closer, a series of practices based on the practical experiences of the performers. Methodologically, the goal of examining practices is to specify the instances of sense-making and situated-ness. Practices illuminate the ways in which actors are able to draw from experience, routine, and shared beliefs about the conduct of governance. Conceiving the practitioners within the ECOWAS Commission as a community of practice places them as agents of governance, responsible for acting out practices and for diffusing the inherent background knowledge of the community across scales of governance. For instance, the practice of holding a training on risk communication in a public health outbreak for public health officials throughout West Africa requires a conscious effort from ECOWAS practitioners to incorporate representatives within the organization and beyond to create a community of actors—in this instance, the community of actors would be media professionals, public health professionals, representatives from Ministries of Health in member states, and so on. By participating in the training, practitioners cultivate a network of relationship with the participants who, in their future interactions with ECOWAS or by virtue of putting their training into practice, are now part of an established pattern of relations, based on similar background dispositions and social context. Hence, trainings sponsored by ECOWAS become iterative actions focused on building epistemic knowledge and a social context where practitioners and other regional actors alike engage in a set of context-specific performances that end up constituting the practice of regional governance.

These practices range from working on the language of trade agreements or visa-free travel provisions, to broader practices such as holding sensitization workshops, networking with or filling governance voids due to policies such as financial decentralization. These practices are considered such because they are patterned, structured interactions that are embedded with social meaning. For example, ECOWAS practitioners often cite the aspiration for the free movement of people in the region as part of ECOWAS' people-centric vision. The collective understanding of what it means to move freely throughout the region is intelligible in specific policies, such as the ECOWAS Brown Card Scheme for regional motor insurance and the Protocol for the Free Movement. These policies resemble an ensemble of skills and background knowledge about the values of the organization, which then are represented through the protocols. In this way, protocols, treaties, and other regional governance agreements are not simply agreements on paper, but are representative of the intersubjective meanings and values of the organization, articulated by the practitioners and agreed upon by the ECOWAS decision makers.

Another reason why practices are a useful analytical framework to examine ECOWAS is due to the ability to attach meaning to the operational aspects of the organization. The focus on adaptation and organizational change is useful for addressing how ECOWAS responds to problems and comes to decide what issues are important. Beyond looking at aspects such as task specialization and the departmental divisions within ECOWAS, this book examines how practitioners identify shifts in the external regional environment and adapt by incorporating new actors and reshaping interactions while existing governance actors process new information. An examination of institutional practices offers a pathway to explain how ECOWAS has expanded and remained durable as an organization, where other perspectives of institutional change would suggest otherwise. The practice framework and the emphasis on ECOWAS practitioners explain why ECOWAS is unique compared to other RECs.

Data and Methodology

To answer the questions posed above, we need to gain insight into practitioners' thoughts and look at the specific practices they engage in. This book examines the conditions in which ECOWAS practitioners engage in regional convergence and how their behaviors condition cohesion in regional governance throughout West Africa. It is not my intent to create a theory of West African integration or African regionalism; rather, I use ECOWAS to examine causal process of how West Africa becomes more coherent as a region. Thus, the purpose of my analysis is to account for the vital observable aspects of regional convergence and make causal inferences on how ECOWAS engages in region-building.

The data collected for this study include original and secondary data. The original data draw from fieldwork conducted in five West African countries: Nigeria, Ghana, Togo, Burkina Faso, and Liberia between 2016 and 2019. This includes over 125 open-ended and structured interviews with officials in the ECOWAS Commission.[18] Other open-ended interviews took place with officials in the West African Civil Society Institute (WACSI), the West African Civil Society Forum (WACSOF), the Kofi Annan International Peacekeeping Training Centre (KAIPTC), ECOWAS Bank of Investment and Development (EBID), the Center of Democracy and Development (CDD) in Nigeria and Ghana, and the West African Health Organization (WAHO), among others. I describe the sites of these interviews in more detail in each of the chapters. Other primary and original data come from archival research conducted from 2016 to 2019 at the ECOWAS Commission library in Abuja, Nigeria; the ECOWAS Parliament in Abuja, Nigeria; the National Defense College in Abuja, Nigeria, EBID in Lomé, Togo, and the World Health Organization (WHO) in Geneva, Switzerland. I compliment the primary source research and interview data with policy documents written by ECOWAS and policies by member state national governments. The analysis is also broadened by a review of scholarly literature on comparative regionalism, international relations theory, peace and security, global health governance, and historical institutionalism.

I use process tracing to examine and explain how officials use the practices of convergence and make inferences about regional connectivity. I also use process tracing to gain historical context to help explain outcomes and gain knowledge as to why regional convergence is occurring. By examining ECOWAS' founding arguments, I show how emerging practices shape the mandate of ECOWAS, and how those arguments create conditions that lead to harmonization. One might also interpret the methodological approach here to approximate what Pouliot calls "practice-tracing." The analysis aims to locate causality in a local context (convergence in West Africa) that could potentially yield analytically general insights.[19] The emphasis on tracing practices provides intelligible evidence of meaning-making through concrete, iterated actions within ECOWAS. By tracing process and practice, I capture the social context of the activities from the level of ECOWAS practitioners, hoping to capture the intersubjective meanings of engagement.

Focusing on the causal relationships between regional activities and regional convergence is important in West Africa and ECOWAS because it enables an inquiry into contextual information that is often treated in passing in other studies of regionalism in Africa. The aim of tracing practices is to move beyond a descriptive analysis of regional organizational activity and illuminate how practices' social context conditions the process of convergence and agency in ECOWAS.

Outline of the Book

What follows is a framework for explaining the process of convergence and agency in ECOWAS. Chapter 2 provides an overview of the framework used to examine convergence and agency in West Africa. The chapter combines practice theory, comparative regionalism, and social and historical institutionalism perspectives to explain how the founding arguments of ECOWAS shape its institutional development. In this argument, the chapter demonstrates how the process of argumentation inherent in the organization's founding created a context where ECOWAS becomes institutionally malleable. The chapter explores the cumulative effects of early institutional innovations in ECOWAS, which help explain later institutional developments, serving as the basis of background knowledge for practitioners.

Chapter 3 details convergence and agency in peace and security. The chapter argues that the context of peace and security governance in West Africa derives from an implicit understanding of the noninterference norm. While there is a strict norm of noninterference between the African countries that informs the insistence of democracy and good governance norms on the continent, ECOWAS was the first entity to intervene in the affairs of a member state officially when it sent troops to Liberia in 1990. This is often considered the starting point of the practice of intervention within West Africa. This chapter makes the argument that part of the founding conditions of ECOWAS was that the member states did not solidify a collective understanding and approach to noninterference from the start, and because of this, they ended up converging around ideas of permissible intervention. Put differently, though there was initially a lack of consensus in what it means for ECOWAS to intervene in the organization, the evolution of the practice of intervention over time has led to a common understanding of how ECOWAS handles security issues in the region. Diversity in the meaning of noninterference eventually evolves to practitioners clearly defining the conditions of intervention and what is permissible by the organization.

Chapter 4 focuses on regional public health governance in West Africa. In this chapter, I examine the process in which ECOWAS practitioners have used networking as a practice to generate harmonization in the region. I focus on two external governance initiatives in West Africa—the Bamako

Initiative in 1987 and the Abuja Declaration in 2001 where WHO and United Nations International Children's Emergency Funds (UNICEF), in conjunction with African Ministers of Health agreed to develop comprehensive strategies to increase access to primary health care by creating minimum health care packages that met community health needs.[20] In this chapter, I find that approaches such as the Bamako Initiative and the Abuja Declaration, though originating from West African states, suffer from top-down projections on how health infrastructure should look. Concurrently, the emergence of public health crises such as the Ebola Virus Disease outbreak in 2014 and later the novel COVID-19 pandemic in 2020 necessitated a coordinated, network response from ECOWAS practitioners and started the process toward institutional change in regional health policy, institutionalized and shaped by ECOWAS practitioners in WAHO to create a coherent and responsive regional health infrastructure. The chapter highlights how WAHO acquires agency as a specialized organ of ECOWAS by building strategic partnerships across scales of governance to both respond to emergencies and create resourceful pathways toward sustainable health governance.

Chapter 5 explores convergence and agency through the relationship between ECOWAS and public and private financial actors in West Africa. Here, I highlight how member state financial deregulation and the reduction of the state's administrative capacity have created an opening for ECOWAS to engage in public–private partnerships to develop private, region-centered financial authority.[21] The chapter explains how ECOWAS practitioners navigate and initiate public–private partnerships and how they contribute to financialization becoming an institutional feature of regional fiscal governance.[22] The chapter shows that the response by ECOWAS to national member state governments giving responsibilities to lower levels of government created a space for ECOWAS and other West African-owned private entities to conduct business throughout the region and lead to the emergence of new private actors and private authority and encouraged convergence through the creation of the ECOWAS Business Incubator for the Advancement of Women Entrepreneurs (ECOWAS BIAWE). I look at the convergence process in the financial institutions of ECOWAS—Ecobank, ECOWAS Business Council, and ECOWAS Business forum, particularly the process in which Ecobank has become the regional investment firm not only for member states but also for other individual investors in Africa. By tracing financialization, I highlight how these firms define the region as the centerpiece of their investment decisions and consider regional culture and identity essential when investing.[23]

In the concluding chapter, I discuss the book's findings and offer implications on what convergence and agency mean to the conduct of region-building in West Africa. I conclude the book by offering some prospects for region-building in the context of extant political controversies in the ECOWAS region. I also raise normative questions about the claim of people-centric governance in the context of West Africa, in the face of growing repression by some ECOWAS member state governments.

Notes

1 Herbst, Jeffrey (2007). "Crafting Regional Cooperation in Africa," in Amitav Acharya and Alastair Iain Johnston, eds. *Crafting Cooperation: Regional International Institutions in Comparative Perspective*. Cambridge University Press.

2 Hartmann, Christof (2016). "Sub-Saharan Africa," in *Oxford Handbook of Comparative Regionalism*, 283; Cissokho, Lassana, Jonathan Haughton, Kossi Makpayo, and Abdoulaye Seck (2013).

"Why Is Agricultural Trade within ECOWAS So High?" *Journal of African Economies* 22(1): 22–51; Yang, Yongzheng and Sanjeev Gupta (2007). "Regional Trade Arrangements in Africa: Past Performance and the Way Forward." *African Development Review* 19(3): 399–431.

3 "West African Regional Bloc Faces Harmonisation Tests" (2019, June 7). Oxford Analytica Daily Brief; Shadows of the Past, Divergent Institutional Futures: Explaining ASEAN's and ECOWAS' Different Approaches to Noninterference with Alice D. Ba; Marshall, Monty G. (2005). "Conflict Trends in Africa." Report prepared for Africa Conflict Prevention Pool, Government of the United Kingdom.

4 Söderbaum, Fredrik (2004). "Modes of Regional Governance in Africa: Neoliberalism, Sovereignty-Boosting and Shadow Networks." *Global Governance: A Review of Multilateralism and International Organizations* 10(4): 419–436; Welz, Martin (2013). *Integrating Africa: Decolonization's Legacies, Sovereignty, and the African Union*. Routledge.

5 Söderbaum describes this process as "shadow governance," which refers to a state where the formal façade of political power is based on informal markets and other entities to shelter corrupt leaders. The proclivity for states to join regional organizations to engage in shadow activities depends on the states' lack of transparency and suggests that heads of states use regional organizations and policy frameworks to further their own interests.

6 Edozie, Rita Kiki and Keith Gottschalk (2014). *The African Union's Africa: New Pan-African Initiatives in Global Governance*. Michigan State University Press.

7 Tieku, Thomas Kwasi and Tanzeel F. Hakak (2014). "A Curious Case of Hybrid Paternalism: Conceptualizing the Relationship Between the UN and AU on Peace and Security." *African Conflict and Peacebuilding Review* 4(2): 129–156.

8 Regionness, coined by Hettne and Söderbaum (2000) refers to the "process whereby a geographical area is transformed from a passive object to an active subject capable of articulating the transnational interests of the emerging region" and explains the social cohesion of a region to the point where it is conceived as an international actor.

9 Glas, Aarie and Emmanuel Balogun (2020). "Norms in Practice: People-centric Governance in ASEAN and ECOWAS." *International Affairs* 96(4): 1015–1032.

10 Acharya, Amitav and Alastair Iain Johnston (2007). *Crafting Cooperation: Regional International Institutions in Comparative Perspective*. Cambridge University Press.

11 Shaw, Timothy M., J. Andrew Grant, and Scarlett Cornelissen (2011). *The Ashgate Research Companion to Regionalisms*. Ashgate.

12 Ba, Alice D. (2009). *(Re) Negotiating East and Southeast Asia: Region, Regionalism, and the Association of Southeast Asian Nations*. Stanford University Press.

13 Ibid.

14 For similar conceptualizations relating to the importance of practitioners, see Glas, A. (2018). "African Union Security Culture in Practice: African Problems and African Solutions." *International Affairs* 94(5): 1121–1138; and Kwesi Tieku, Thomas (2018). *Governing Africa: 3D Analysis of the African Union's Performance*. Rowman & Littlefield.

15 Bueger, Christian and Frank Gadinger (2015). "The Play of International Practice." *International Studies Quarterly* 59(10): 449–460; Pouliot, Vincent and Jérémie Cornut (2015). "Practice Theory and the Study of Diplomacy: A Research Agenda." *Cooperation and Conflict* 50(3): 297–315.

16 Interview, ECOWAS official, Emergency Response Team, October 16, 2016, Abuja, Nigeria.

17 Kay, Sean (1998). *NATO and the Future of European Security*. Lanham, MD: Rowman & Littlefield; Tallberg, Jonas (2000). "The Anatomy of Autonomy: An Institutional Account of Variation in Supranational Influence." *Journal of Common Market Studies* 38(5): 843–864; Yi-Chong, Xu and Patrick Weller (2008). " 'To Be, But not to Be Seen': Exploring the Impact of International Civil Servants." *Public Administration* 86(1): 35–51.

18 The interviews conducted at the ECOWAS Commission took place in the following departments: External Relations, Directorate of Early Warning, The Financial Controller of ECOWAS Institutions; Macroeconomic Policy and Economic Research, Political Affairs Peace and Security, Social Affairs and Gender, Trade Custom, and Free Trade, and Education, Science, and Culture.

19 Pouliot, Vincent (2015). "Practice-Tracing." In *Process Tracing From Metaphor to Analytical Tool*, eds. Andrew Bennett and Jeffery T. Checkel. Cambridge University Press.

20 The Bamako initiative, in particular, demonstrated a commitment to community participation in health management and making health care affordable to citizens. Success with these initiatives was contingent on West African countries engaging in the proper political processes to facilitate these changes.

21 The World Bank defines fiscal deregulation as

> a) self-financing or cost recovery through user charges, b) co-financing or co-production arrangements through which the users participate in providing services and infrastructure through monetary or labor contributions; c) expansion of local revenues through property or sales taxes, or indirect charges; d) intergovernmental transfers that shift general revenues from taxes collected by the central government to local governments for general or specific uses; and e) authorization of municipal borrowing and the mobilization of either national or local government resources through loan guarantees.

22 Financialization is defined as the increasing importance of financial markets, financial motives, financial institutions, and financial elites in the operation of the economy and its governing institutions at the local and national levels.

23 For more on this important point of West African–centric investment, see Iheduru, Okechukwu C. (2012). "Regional Integration and the Private Authority of Banks in West Africa." *International Studies Review* 14(2): 273–302. DOI: 10.1111/j.1468-2486.2012.01112.x

Bibliography

Acharya, Amitav and Alastair Iain Johnston. 2007. Crafting Cooperation: Regional International Institutions in Comparative Perspective. Cambridge University Press.

Ba, Alice D. 2009. (Re) Negotiating East and Southeast Asia: Region, Regionalism, and the Association of Southeast Asian Nations. Stanford University Press.

Ba, Alice D. and Monty G. Marshall. 2005. "Conflict Trends in Africa." Report prepared for Africa Conflict Prevention Pool, Government of the United Kingdom.

Bueger, Christian and Frank Gadinger. 2015. "The Play of International Practice." International Studies Quarterly 59(10): 449–460.

Cissokho, Lassana, Jonathan Haughton, Kossi Makpayo, and Abdoulaye Seck. 2013. "Why Is Agricultural Trade within ECOWAS So High?" Journal of African Economies 22(1): 22–51.

Edozie, Rita Kiki and Keith Gottschalk. 2014. The African Union's Africa: New Pan-African Initiatives in Global Governance. Michigan State University Press.

Emergency Response Team. 2016, October 16. Interview, ECOWAS official. Abuja, Nigeria.

Glas, Aarie. 2018. "African Union Security Culture in Practice: African Problems and African Solutions." International Affairs 94(5): 1121–1138.

Glas, Aarie and Emmanuel Balogun. 2020. "Norms in Practice: People-centric Governance in ASEAN and ECOWAS." International Affairs 96(4): 1015–1032.

Grant, Andrew and Söderbaum, Fredrik. 2003. The New Regionalism in Africa. Aldershot: Ashgate.

Hartmann, Christof. 2016. "Sub-Saharan Africa." In Oxford Handbook of Comparative Regionalism, eds. Tanja Borzel and Thomas Risse. New York, NY: Oxford University Press, 271–294.

Herbst, Jeffrey. 2000. States and Power in Africa. Princeton University Press.

Herbst, Jeffrey. 2007. "Crafting Regional Cooperation in Africa." In Crafting Cooperation: Regional International Institutions in Comparative Perspective, eds. Amitav Acharya and Alastair Iain Johnston. Cambridge University Press.

Hettne, Bjorn and Fredrik Söderbaum. 2000. "Theorising the Rise of Regionness." New Political Economy 5(3): 457–472. DOI: 10.1080/713687778

Iheduru, Okechukwu C. 2012. "Regional Integration and the Private Authority of Banks in West Africa." International Studies Review 14(2): 273–302. DOI: 10.1111/j.1468-2486.2012.01112.x

Kay, Sean. 1998. NATO and the Future of European Security. Lanham, MD: Rowman & Littlefield.

Oxford Analytica Daily Brief. 2019, June 7. West African Regional Bloc Faces Harmonisation Tests.

Pouliot, Vincent. 2015. "Practice-Tracing." In Process Tracing From Metaphor to Analytical Tool, eds. Andrew Bennett and Jeffery T. Checkel. Cambridge University Press.

Pouliot, Vincent and Jérémie Cornut. 2015. "Practice Theory and the Study of Diplomacy: A Research Agenda." Cooperation and Conflict 50(3): 297–315.

Shaw, Timothy M., J. Andrew Grant, and Scarlett Cornelissen. 2011. The Ashgate Research Companion to Regionalisms. Ashgate.

Söderbaum, Fredrik. 2004. "Modes of Regional Governance in Africa: Neoliberalism, Sovereignty-Boosting and Shadow Networks." Global Governance: A Review of Multilateralism and International Organizations 10(4): 419–436.

Tallberg, Jonas. 2000. "The Anatomy of Autonomy: An Institutional Account of Variation in Supranational Influence." Journal of Common Market Studies 38(5): 843–864.

Tieku, Thomas Kwasi. 2018. Governing Africa: 3D Analysis of the African Union's Performance. Rowman & Littlefield.

Tieku, Thomas Kwasi and Tanzeel F. Hakak. 2014. "A Curious Case of Hybrid Paternalism: Conceptualizing the Relationship Between the UN and AU on Peace and Security." African Conflict and Peacebuilding Review 4(2): 129–156.

Villalón, Leonardo A., and Peter VonDoepp, eds. 2005. The Fate of Africa's Democratic Experiments: Elites and Institutions. Indiana University Press.

Welz, Martin. 2013. Integrating Africa: Decolonization's Legacies, Sovereignty, and the African Union. Routledge.

Yang, Yongzheng and Sanjeev Gupta. 2007. "Regional Trade Arrangements in Africa: Past Performance and the Way Forward." African Development Review 19(3): 399–431.

Yi-Chong, Xu and Patrick Weller. 2008. "'To Be, But not to Be Seen': Exploring the Impact of International Civil Servants." Public Administration 86(1): 35–51.

2 Conceptualizing Convergence and Agency in ECOWAS

The process of creating Economic Community of West African States (ECOWAS) took over 15 years, as Heads of State in West Africa stressed the importance of economic integration toward the stability of West Africa; political instability, extra-African influence, and the potential of large state dominance in the region loomed large as stumbling blocks to integration. In the years that followed the organization's founding, the view about ECOWAS has been that it has struggled on the front of economic integration while shifting to becoming an organization focused on political, social, and cultural integration. What accounts for this change in organizational focus? How has ECOWAS persisted given the differences in interest, lineage, and material capacities among member states?

To explain the processes of convergence and agency related to ECOWAS' institutional development, I explain how the founding arguments that led to the creation of ECOWAS inform later institutional developments. The founding ideas and logic of ECOWAS' development are contextualized by emphasizing the processes of consensus-building and divergence in the creation of ECOWAS. A focus on founding arguments of ECOWAS' creation takes stock of the practical sense and background knowledge that inform practitioners in the process and the development of organizational culture. These arguments demonstrate constant process of argumentation between actors tasked with building intersubjective meanings of engagement.

The chapter also explores ECOWAS' evolution as an organization and details how the cumulative effects of early institutional innovations help explain institutional developments over time and inform the background conditions of practitioners in the organization.

Finally, the chapter concludes by highlighting the practices of convergence that are at play in ECOWAS: *organizational dynamism* and *networking*. Organizational dynamism emphasizes how the process of argumentation in ECOWAS's founding serves as the source of institutional change made dependable and durable by ECOWAS practitioners. Networking underscores the role and emergence of ECOWAS practitioners, their agency, and the mutually constituted institutional space created for them to be activists and engage in region-building. These convergence practices allow us to locate the

DOI: 10.4324/9780429436734-2

sources of institutional change and identify specific mechanisms of regional convergence.

Defining Region-Building

What is meant by "region-building"? How is it different from regionalization and regionalism? How is it specific to the West African context? Region-building here builds on a definition from De Lombaerde and Van Lagenhove and is defined here as a multidimensional process of social transformation whereby a diversity of actors create networks, based on intense interactions. These iterated interactions result in the creation of new practices, the creation of coordinated or common action policies, and/or the creation of regional institutions, thereby creating a new relevant (regional) space for many aspects of human behavior and activities (Van Langenhove and De Lombaerde 2007).[1] This definition privileges region-building as a process, occurring through intense interactions that deepen connectivity between actors. Understanding region-building as a process of deepening captures and embraces the idea that regional connectivity ought to be embedded in human and regional activities. The definition also implies that region-building is a constructive process that requires a negotiated, intersubjective understanding between actors and places a focal point on the processes of cooperation that link the social and political activity of actors across scales of governance. Region-building then, requires a process of argumentation and contestation to inform the scope of cooperation, rather than constrain cooperation.

Because region-building considers the diversity of actors engaged in regional governance and the scope of their interactions, it also assumes that the actors involved in these processes have agency that enables them to engage in region-building. As such, part of understanding this process of region-building is also to understand how the actors acquire and use their agency to contribute to region-building. How did ECOWAS end up on this path? To answer this, it is worth looking back at West African countries' political context and debates prior to and during the formation of ECOWAS and to take stock in the conceptual debates that characterizes regional governance in West Africa.

Taking Stock of Regional Governance in West Africa

Existing approaches to understanding region-building in West Africa focus on the failures of economic integration and the realpolitik and competition between ECOWAS member states. These approaches include:

- Pooled sovereignty in Postindependence West Africa
- Constraints by the regional hegemon
- Regional cooperation as a resurgence of Pan-Africanism

Each of these arguments assume region-building to be a defensive response meant to consider and protect notions of postcolonial sovereignty and position the drivers of regionalism as extractive and self-interested. However, these approaches do not account for the agential capacity of practitioners, which enhances the ability to look beyond the state as a means to empirically explain region-building in West Africa.

For example, pooled sovereignty, generally understood as a way to "share" sovereignty by states agreeing to give up some of their sovereignty for the collective relies heavily on the assumption that the material conditions of states necessitate trade-offs in security and stability, reductions in military spending, and enhanced economic and technological cooperation (Fioramonti and Mattheis 2016; Moravcsik 1988). Pooling sovereignty also necessitates strong institutions at the national level in cooperating states in order to implement integration arrangements. In addition, ECOWAS is often characterized as being dominated by Nigeria—as evidenced by the common saying among ECOWAS practitioners "when Nigeria coughs, the whole of ECOWAS catches a cold." Nigeria is often characterized as the most important actor in the region because of its size, relative material wealth, and disproportionate contributions to the mandate of ECOWAS. Despite these characterizations, three factors explain why regional hegemon/pooled sovereignty as the main explanation for regional cooperation does not reflect governance in West Africa.

First, assumptions of pooled sovereignty and Nigeria's position as a dominant actor in ECOWAS overestimate the influence Nigeria has over regional and subregional integration efforts. The recent ratification and entry into force of the African Continental Free Trade Agreement (AfCFTA), provides an interesting context. 11 of 15 ECOWAS member states, including Ghana, Senegal, and Cote d'Ivorie, ratified AfCFTA and were among the first 44 countries to sign the agreement. Nigeria, in dramatic fashion, ratified the treaty right before the initial launch date at the African Union (AU) Summit on July 7, 2019. Nigeria was initially reluctant to ratify and enter the treaty because other African countries would take advantage of dumping, which would diminish Nigeria's manufacturing sector (Isah 2018). The fact that the treaty was going to enter into force, with or without Nigeria, indicates that, at least from a macroeconomic perspective, its region-mates are neither constrained nor need or seek buy-in from Nigeria to enter macroeconomic arrangements. Nigeria has been passive in facilitating other regional arrangements within ECOWAS, namely, the ECOWAS Common External Tariff (ECOWAS CET), and has been limited in its capacity to facilitate single currency integration, a project that has since been usurped by France and the Francophone ECOWAS member states in late 2019. Yet, in justifying its protectionist stance against the AfCFTA, Nigerian trade representatives often cite existing trade liberalization schemes in West Africa, such as ECOWAS CET. While Nigeria provides substantial governance resources such as peacekeeping troops and subsidizing community levies, the pooled sovereignty and regional hegemon perspective privileges a materialist understanding of regionalism and region-building that does not account for the activism and agency of market actors and overstates the importance of larger economic powers like Nigeria in facilitating regional integration.

Another potential explanation for regional cooperation in West Africa is the claim that the region-building process in West Africa is part of a broader resurgence of Pan-Africanism as an ideology and logic of integration. Pan-Africanism sentiments related to regionalism often refer to the continental approach promoted by former Ghanaian President and leader, Kwame Nkrumah. Nkrumah, who embraced and promoted Marcus Garvey's "Back to Africa" movement, often cited the need for African countries to be organized in a continental organization that adhered to the principles and ideology of Pan-Africanism. Pan-Africanism is defined as an ideology based on the idea that African people within the continent and abroad all share a common history and identity. Pan-Africanism rests upon the following broad principles:

> Africa as the homeland of Africans and persons of African origin, solidarity among people of African descent, belief in a distinct African personality, rehabilitation of Africa's past, pride in African culture, Africa for Africans in church and state and the hope for a united and glorious future of Africa.

Pan-Africanism is also described as a movement based on unity, solidarity, and collective reliance from the people.[2]

Pan-Africanism in postindependence Africa served as a reclamation project for African leaders and countries to regain control and perspective of the African identity—a project that called for the redemption and realization of people to reconstruct their ideologies and remove the stigmas of colonization. Leaders used Pan-Africanism as a "rallying slogan, a springboard, and an ideological vehicle for cultivating the common efforts of African peoples to advance their political efforts globally" (Edozie and Gottschalk 2014, xxvii). In many ways, leaders use Pan-Africanism as an ideological networking tool, sculpting African identity and agency ideas (see Mumford 2020).

However, while Pan-Africanism, removes the emphasis of the state as the main unit of analysis and allows us to investigate how the ideas and values enter the region-building discourse and is inclusive of a larger collectivity of uniquely African actors and institutions, the explanation breaks down in a couple of ways. First, while practitioners and the Authority Heads of State and Government allude to Pan-African solidarity, there are still those who, despite working for the institution, characterize ECOWAS as a neocolonial institution. So far as the institutions of ECOWAS are there to preserve sovereignty, territorial integrity, and independence of member states, then it could not embody the ideals of Pan-Africanism. Despite the ability for Pan-Africanism to provide context to investigate how practitioners think about Pan-Africanism empirically, its applicability to convergence and agency remains limited. Pan-Africanism serves as a rhetorical, symbolic, or material representation of West African–led political initiatives, yet it remains unclear whether the said representations are iterative, evoke the agentic capacity of practitioners, and illuminate notions of unity and solidarity. Moreover, analyses using Pan-Africanism as a mechanism for cooperation often reflect what Mumford calls the "Pan-African rhetorical trap." The Pan-African rhetorical trap describes a normative environment in which specific outcomes become irresistible for a variety of actors because they accord unambiguously with the norms of the African community.[3]

Shadow regionalism is another perceived constraint to regional cooperation in West Africa. Shadow regionalism is the belief that underlying motivations and strategies guide African participation in regional agreements by ruling regimes, and regionalization is used as an instrument to boost absolute state sovereignty and not the broader interest of society. In this approach, African leaders purposely engage in "shadow" activities to pursue their own interests, without a formal state bureaucracy (Reno 1995). Relying on the assumption of the inherent weakness of African states, West African Heads of State use these shadow activities to enhance power and authority[4] (Clapham 1996; Fanta 2008).

The idea behind shadow regionalism and regime-boosting is that regional arrangements help secure African leaders and ask little in return (Herbst 2009, 144; Söderbaum 2011, 7). One specific example of this is "summitry," when African leaders gather and construct narratives of regional organizations, which "involve no real debate and no wider consultation within or between member states" (Simon 2003, 71; Söderbaum 2011, 7). Summitry frames regional cooperation as a façade, in that Heads of States in West Africa are committed to the front-facing talk of regional cooperation, yet not committed to the actual project of region-building due to the slow process on key integration indicators. However, critiques of summitry do not account for the relational ties created in the informal interactions between leaders at extraordinary summits or the range of practitioners who are often responsible for developing regional governance policy. In short, the frame of summitry, as an example, is another way in which the success or failure of regional integration in West Africa is tethered to the assumption of Heads of State of government as the key actors in region-building.

Shadow regionalism relies on the assumption that African leaders are only out to subvert the regionalism process and that African leaders are intimately involved with all processes of region-building. Relatedly, shadow regionalism underestimates the importance of informal interactions by non-state/sub-state actors at the "meso-level" of regional analysis, where practitioners are the primary interlocutors. Intensified informal interactions or the unofficial stances taken outside of the formal locales of regional organizations are not necessarily subversive; rather, these informal interactions are part of a broader repertoire of practices employed by practitioners that drive convergence.

Concepts like shadow regionalism limit the ability to examine how other relevant stakeholders are included into the region-building project. Specifically, state/society relations as it pertains to region-building are often framed as purely transactional, in that citizens of Africa are beholden to bargaining situations with "big-men" who can provide basic needs that they might not typically have access to, such as medicine in rural areas. The society side of the equation never possesses agentic qualities and has no choice but to engage in neopatrimonial behavior, which renders civil society organizations irrelevant or ineffectual as part of region-building. Hence, it is necessary in a process, practice-oriented approach to region-building in West Africa, to look at the ways in which civil society and their strategic interactions with ECOWAS have led to the development of a more inclusive regional governance space where civil society actors are not agent-less in a transactional, hierarchical relationship with the state, but are also part of the active construction of the ideas, behaviors, and practices that shape the complexion of the region.

Processes of convergence and agency in West Africa consider how the networking of "informal" actors is not meant to (only) boost the legitimacy of otherwise illegitimate West African leaders; rather, it is to help identify specific stakeholders that are inclined to cultivate cross-cultural ties. Another key distinction is in the assumption that the informal, noninstitutionalized interactions characterized by shadow regionalism operate outside of the regional organizations. The approach offered here examines the ways in which ECOWAS engages intentionally or unintentionally, directly or indirectly, with actors classified as "informal."[5]

While the components of African regionalism mentioned above are tied to assumptions about the African state and its constitutive parts, the governance turn in comparative regionalism encourages scholars to emphasize and broaden the scope of regional cooperation past viewing and thinking of regionalism as merely an interstate project (Börzel 2016, 53). The governance turn accentuates civil society and market actors' role and process and provides a framework for comparing the institutional settings in which these actors coordinate. Governance in comparative regionalism takes three forms: hierarchy, market, and networks (Börzel 2016, 53).

Analytically, the focus on governance is helpful to incorporate civil society actors and actors in the "ungoverned" spaces within the region. Governance as a frame becomes important when accounting for the diminishing role of governments within the region, or when considering the activities and actions of actors outside of the purview of the government. A useful conception of governance includes systems of rule at all levels of human activity—from the family to international organization in which the pursuit of goals through the exercise of control has transnational repercussions (Dingwerth and Pattberg 2006; Rosenau 2002).

However, the focus on governance broadly might only yield insight on how regional structures are preferentially ordered, how rules of regional integration are structured, and the how the interaction between the formal and the informal shape the outcome and effectiveness of regional governance. A broad conception of the role of governance on regional cooperation does little to inform us about the background knowledge that actors use to construct the rules of governance or how the interactions between multiple actors, across spheres of governance, connect to make governance rules, practices, and norms intelligible to across scales of governance. The network governance approach is a possible pathway toward understanding how governance can account for the convergence of political actors in a given region.

Network governance approaches identify specific non-state actors and civil society stakeholders who are typically removed from regionalization analysis. Ohanyan (2014, 3–6), in her analysis of conflict management in politically divided areas, examines which actors are pushing toward conflict management and how relationships between regional actors are cultivated locally (Ohanyan 2014). Ohanyan also highlights the structural composition of networks to reveal interests driving regional formation and questions if the institutional make up of a region conditions prospects of conflict management. Taking a network approach bolsters the necessity to look at regional building from the bottom-up and considers institutional composition's role in regional building. Put differently, a networked approach engages the process of region convergence, its conditions, and how it informs us how the process and conditions of convergence contribute to the complexion of the region.

Contesting Region-Building Through Argumentation

One of the first justifications for considering a union between West African states began during the Nigerian Civil War in 1966–1970, where General Yakubu Gowon of Nigeria argued that domestic consolidation of the countries in the region, especially Nigeria's, was crucial to any efforts of regional integration. Gowon argued that the lack of unified West African countries and a "strong and united Nigeria" would rob Africa of an influential and respected voice in international affairs. General Gowon also argued that civil wars were tests of "diplomacy" and the Nigerian Civil War would test the loyalty of the former French colonies in the region that were under pressure from the former colonial power to pick a side in the secessionist movement in Nigeria.

These ideas point to the different ways West African leaders perceived the postindependence landscape and underscored the contested idea of what a "West African" region would look like. As Nigeria's civil war illuminates, the postcolonial West African state was itself a contested idea, complicated by a desire by postcolonial African leaders such as Kwame Nkrumah to "respect the independence, sovereignty, and territorial integrity" of other African states, inherently embracing colonial operational and bureaucratic practices. Further, notions of pan-regional or pan-territorial identity were also elusive, evidenced by the failure of colonial federations such as the Afrique occidentale Française (AOF) and the Afrique équatorial Française (AEF) to generate postcolonial unity or regional identity (Young 2012). The development of the Organization of African Unity (OAU) was the most symbolic notion of an idea of Pan-Africanism, and early Pan-Africanist advocates sought to rally around shared experiences of colonialism to deepen claims and calls for solidarity; however, calls for solidarity and African unity were often placed in tension with principles of sovereignty and territorial integrity that superseded notions of collectivity.

For example, France and Côte d'Ivoire toyed with the idea of commenting and condemning Nigeria. However, Cote d'Ivoire and Nigeria were also part of the OAU, and the charter adhered members to principles of noninterference while asserting the rights to self-determination of African peoples. Other West African States such as Niger, Mali, and Upper Volta (current day Burkina Faso) were initially unequivocal in their opposition to recognizing Biafra and aligned with Gowon's perception of the importance of a unified Nigeria. For instance, in a newspaper article from 1968, former President of Mali, Modibo Keita, stated that it was "inconsistent" for African countries to support secessionist movements when countries are trying to create more coherent and larger groupings. The breakup of Nigeria, according to Keita, would set a "serious precedent" for the political unity of African countries. Keita further argued that Mali believed in the process of creating a unified African grouping, and that governments should not encourage secession on a "tribal basis."

Côte d'Ivorie did not initially comment on the secessionist movement, and it was not until Julius Nyerere of Tanzania's open support and recognition of Biafra as an "independent" and "sovereign" entity that Cote d'Ivoire came out as the only West African state to recognize Biafra as a sovereign state. President Felix Houphouet-Boigny of Cote d'Ivoire justified his recognition of Biafra by arguing that it was "utopian" to believe that Nigeria, based on its large size and population, could ever be consolidated. Cote d'Ivoire's skepticism about Nigeria's ability to consolidate was also informed by its own aspirations to lead and establish regional francophone organizations with significant partnerships with France.

A glimpse into attempts at regional integration between former French colonies also illuminates a history of argumentation and contestation. Many of the former French West African colonies entered into cooperation agreements with France at the time of independence centered on a concerted approach in French–West African relations with the European Community. Francophone West African countries established common policies that resulted in direct linkages to France, and these policies were tailored to meet national development needs and to consolidate intra-francophone relations (Bach 1995). The French took an active role in establishing administrative and institutional cooperation at independence to, from their vantage point, fill in the gaps of human resource, compensate for the lack of economic viability by the newly independent states, and establish political and administrative continuity.

While it may certainly be the case that the French have had a heavy presence in attempting to forge unity between its former colonies in West Africa, and while one would assume that the shared experience of French colonialism and the retention and embrace of French presence would preclude harmonization among Francophone West African states, the reality was that the idea of a French West Africa was highly contested. For example, the creation of the Mali Federation, which contained Senegal, French Sudan, Dahomey (Benin), and Upper Volta (Burkina Faso), provoked a counter group by Cote d'Ivoire and Niger, with the support from France. From the counter group, Upper Volta and Dahomey leave the Mali Federation and create the Conseil de l'Entente with Niger and Cote d'Ivoire, with Togo joining in 1966. Leaders of the Conseil de l'Entente suggest that this grouping, and its support from France, is meant to counter the regional agenda of Kwame Nkrumah of Ghana. The Conseil de l'Entente gave more power to Houphouet-Boigny and Cote d'Ivoire as a legitimate challenge to Nigeria's burgeoning material power in the region and also posed an ideological challenge to the Pan-African politics and ideology of Nkrumah. These configurations were also part of broader attempts of Francophone African unity, particularly through the Union Africaine et Malgache and the OCAM. In practice, the organizations were extensions of bilateral linkages with France, particularly considering that France's policy was to isolate or destabilize countries that attempted to undermine their policy of consolidating Franco-African relations (Bach 1995).

Considering the politics and contested ideas around Francophone West African integration and cooperation, Cote d'Ivoire's support of Biafra, despite the failure of its secession efforts, becomes crucial in understanding the different ways actors see the region being cut, even among allies. Cote d'Ivoire's tactical, yet deliberate support of a secessionist movement in Nigeria foreshadowed the tensions African countries would face in the postindependence era, namely, appeasing extra-regional actors (such as France), preserving ideas of sovereignty as the "sacrosanct principle of inter-African affairs" (Taylor 2013), and competing notions of solidarity. The recognition of Biafra also signaled that the contestation over ideas of West Africa would also be based on postcolonial agreements and politics made by Nigeria and Cote d'Ivoire, and their former colonial powers, England and France, respectively. Another example of the contestation around the idea of a postcolonial unified West Africa was the creation of an alliance or entente between Nigeria and other Francophone states who objected the recognition of Biafra, but also believed that it would not be in the interest of West African unity to have a constant state of civil conflict inflicting the region. As members of the entente, President Senghor of Senegal pushed for mediation in the Nigerian civil war and Sekou Touré of Guinea openly criticized Houphouet-Boigny for trying to coordinate a campaign in West Africa to recognize and support Biafra.

As the example of the Nigerian civil war and the attempts of Francophone West African integration illustrate, it was common practice for regional leaders at the time to comment on the affairs of other nations, and more broadly, these developments offered new opportunities for newly independent states to determine the scope of regional cooperation and organization. Ideologically, leaders in postcolonial West Africa believed it to be a necessity to retain a relationship with their former colonizers, while also deeming cooperation necessary to secure and protect the cause of African unity. We see this through the tension in Cote d'Ivoire's position as the only country at the end of the Nigerian Civil War to actively support and engage in the recognition of Biafra, while its other allies in the AOF and OCAM, who were also members of the entente, were actively against it, for fears that it would jeopardize a prospective inclusive West African grouping. Argumentation and contestation between postindependence West African states is a defining characteristic of the founding logics that underlie regional cooperation in West Africa.

The process of argumentation between West African countries prior to the founding of ECOWAS indicates how regional cooperation in West Africa is historically conditioned, while also providing a pathway to examine other avenues to cooperation. Argumentation and contestation are typically perceived as factors that constrain cooperation. Take, for example, accounts of regionalism that concern themselves with actor preferences and preference formation based on internal ruling coalitions within the state (Mansfield and Solingen 2010; Moravcsik and Schimmelfennig 2009). These arguments suggest that states with dissimilar institutions have much to gain by cooperating, but are constrained because the impediments to do so are too substantial. More broadly, approaches that consider contestation and structural differences as impediments to cooperation suggest that domestic politics and regime types matter, as it takes a strong domestic coalition for states to buy into the benefits of regional cooperation (Katzenstein 2005; Solingen 2008). Even in attempts to understand regionalism that is inclusive to the role non-state actors play in regional integration, the focus has remained on constraints to regional cooperation, particularly in developing countries. However, uncovering the substance and process of argumentation in ECOWAS' founding amends for this focus on the constraints to cooperation and, instead, emphasizes the points of disagreement and the process with which actors can agree.

How then does one conceptualize region-building informed by identity, unity and substantive diversity among regional actors, and institution building and evolution? In building this conceptual framework, it is important to understand how historical argumentation processes inform the habits and behaviors of actors within institutions, practices that emerge from these processes, and how those practices allow actors to acquire agency. A process-driven focus on region-building considers regional activity—dynamic or dormant, stable or unstable, and everything in between, as part of the habits and practices of a regional organization. A process-driven account also broadens the sphere of regional activity to be inclusive of the interactions across the depth of a regional network to better understand linkages and relationships.

Understanding Practices: Toward a Practitioner-Led Regionalism

If regional actors are constrained by argumentation, what prompts regional cooperation among actors with persistent, divergent interests and relations? Take, for instance, the proliferation of gangs, drugs, viruses, and epidemics, all of which directly impact West African states and societies, issues that require responses.[6] Against this backdrop, harmonization processes can be constrained by the unevenness of capacity and material capability between West African states to respond to these issue areas adequately. However, instead of emphasizing West Africa's inability to overcome systemic constraints, to understand cooperation between diverse actors and idea requires a perspective that stratifies the diversity of linkages between society, state, and region, while emphasizing how those linkages lead to the emergence and importance of new actors that change the context of cooperation. Incorporating linkages between society, state, and region despite differences in capabilities and ideas is central to region-building.

The region-building processes in West Africa shift the focus of regionalism in Africa toward an emphasis on the composition of actors, how they acquire agency, and the significance of the relationships they form with other regional actors. A common characterization of African regionalism focuses on the "weakness" of domestic institutions, a desire to "pool sovereignty" or the persistence of overlapping memberships to regional institutions. By defining and understanding region-building as a process with a multitude of diverse and agentic actors, we can begin to understand the durability of ECOWAS as an organization. Additionally, the region-building process explains the driving forces behind the style of interaction between actors within West Africa across scales of governance—from civil society and grassroots groups, to bureaucrats within ECOWAS, to the leaders of West African countries. Understanding region-building in West Africa through examining practices within ECOWAS helps measure identity, indicate how ideas are widely shared throughout West Africa, and how much these ideas of identity and region-building relate to or deviate from factors of African regionalism.[7] Focusing on the processes of region-building in West Africa, we can begin to rethink the conventionally self-interested and material driven concepts typically associated with African regionalism, notably, concepts such as regime-boosting and shadow regionalism.[8]

Because ECOWAS is an intergovernmental organization, most evaluations of its effectiveness or its utility focus on the political will of member states to engage in regional harmonization. ECOWAS progress on regional integration appeared to be part of the "politics of illusion" due to a lack of political will by Heads of States to implement policies in their member states, weak institutional capacity in the organization, and the persistence of political rivalries between regional leaders (Iheduru 2011). However, as studies of micro-regionalism suggest, it is necessary to situate the agency of African actors into a broader context of the overlapping and interconnected dynamics between African states and society (Söderbaum and Taylor 2008).

One way to understand region-building and harmonization beyond the role of Heads of States is to consider the role of international bureaucrats or practitioners. Practitioners are often the public face of international organizations and play a prominent role in shaping regional agendas serving as "policy initiators" able to demonstrate agency, autonomy, and independence in overcoming traditional hurdles to regional cooperation such as state capacity and political will (Tieku 2017).

Practitioners are significant to region-building in several ways. First, practitioners mediate contestation over institutional rules, values, and resources. Practitioners use their background knowledge of the organization to demonstrate how they can bring the region together through institutional maintenance, networking with peer institutions, and understanding and working through institutional constraints. Thus, practitioners are crucial for the maintenance and durability of ECOWAS, due to their ability to create norms through their involvement in policy creation and initiation. Practitioners may also reproduce or acknowledge extant norms and belief systems in the organization and contest these existing norms in the organization.

The behaviors and performances of practitioners in ECOWAS are signs of the agency afforded to bureaucratic actors and their ability to take into account the cultural contexts of the organization to create patterned practices and routines that dictate the scope and depth of interactions between ECOWAS and regional stakeholders. Practitioners rely on these iterative interactions to normalize relations between member states and between the organization and regional stakeholders such as non-governmental organizations (NGOs) and civil society.

Practices are meaningful because they enable agency by transforming background knowledge into intentional acts with social meaning, while background knowledge and practices in general do not assume uniformity or monolithic understandings of actors within the community of practice, defined here as relatively bounded groups of actors united and observable through their shared repertoires of action, common enterprise, and dense interactions (Bueger 2019; Glas 2018; Glas and Balogun 2020). Background knowledge provides a sense and understanding of how actors interpret their agency and also how they acquire agency.

The competent acts of ECOWAS practitioners provide an analytical framework to demonstrate how we can isolate agency to not just focus on abstract criteria such as "the state" or "international institutions," but to focus on how socially meaningful "ways of doing" are positioned in a local, social environment (Balogun 2021; Adler-Nissen and Drieschova 2019). Understanding practices as both ideational and material, as well as acknowledging their reinforcing character, indicates how practices both shape rules and institutions and can transform those same rules and institutions. Practices allow us to isolate and specify the unit of analysis, assuming that an actor's subjective experiences form the starting point of any analysis (Adler and Pouliot 2011).

Practices are often linked relationally with agency and structure. The relational dynamics of structure and agency is well documented in constructivist and practice theory literature; however, practice theory aims to liberate agency from the constrictions of structure (Bueger 2019). A focus on practice and agency becomes a focus on the meaning of action. Put differently, by focusing on the meanings of actions, we can examine how actors acquire and use agency. As Bueger notes, this leads to an understanding of agency as distributed—an agency dependent on webs of relations, which help discern the scope of engagements which lead actors to acquire agency. Agency in this conception is not given, it is acquired through participation in practices (Bueger 2019, 835).

What are some of the practices—the everyday, routinized interactions of practitioners, that contribute to the institutional maintenance of ECOWAS? How do practitioner activities become normalized? What are the ways in which practitioners understand their institutional contexts and constraints? Broadly, institutional practices can come in the form of diplomatic text production, holding of summits, renegotiating institutional rules and norms, or an aggregate of all of these practices and more (Adler and Pouliot 2011). ECOWAS practitioners engage in these practices; however, I focus on two particular practices that drive the process of region-building in West Africa—*networking* and what I call *organizational dynamism*.

Networking as Practice

The practitioners within ECOWAS can be conceptualized as a "community of practice." ECOWAS practitioners are considered a discrete group of officials bound together by common enterprise, dense interactions, and shared tools and resources with which they pursue their goals (Bueger 2017; Glas and Balogun 2020). As a community of practice, extra-community norms are confronted and constructed to fit existing organizational characteristics, including established notions of efficacy and appropriateness. Through the practice of networking, ECOWAS officials can capture new avenues of resource accumulation, exhibit autonomy in their decision-making in who engages with the organization and on what terms, and implement decisions based on mutually constituted rules and procedures, that potentially deviate from the political stances of politically appointed leaders.

Networking as practice refers to the multitude of repertories and activities practitioners engage in to bring regional stakeholders into the governance. The act of networking by practitioners can and often does vary—from deeply integrated interactions and relationships with actors, to narrowly defined partnerships with specific actors. Networking as a practice can vary in terms of density, the amount of linkages created between ECOWAS and regional partners, and the scope of which these networks can permeate into member state policies. Networking as a practice is also primarily issue-based—meaning that ECOWAS practitioners often engage in networking as a means to engage with one or a couple of specific issue areas that are relevant to advancing the cause of region-building. The ends of networking as a practice might implicate a number of different policy areas, but the scope of the networking is usually narrowly focused.

How do practitioners engage in networking? Practitioners use a number of methods to engage in networking and can manifest through means that are commonly associated with the actions and activities of regional organizations and also in ways that are specific to the organizational context. For instance, some common networking practices range from the construction and negotiating of memorandums of understanding, to holding sensitization workshops, to facilitating joint statements and courtesy visits with national governments and formal modes of regional integration, such as the establishment of free-trade areas and the creation of currency unions. In terms of "informal" modes of integration, the networking practices are often part of the process of creating transnational civil society and advocacy networks, trade corridors, and triangles.

By engaging in networking, practitioners are able to demonstrate their agency in governance processes and policy initiation. For instance, practitioners use the resources from networking to create frameworks to deal with health emergencies or coordinate on best practices related to health interventions. Or practitioners might use the practice of networking to facilitate election monitoring, to create harmonization strategies, or to develop standard operating procedures relating to military intervention or mediation within a member state. Practitioners can also use networks to clearly define the scope of public–private partnerships, considering the dynamic relationships between business actors or civil society actors and member states. Networking as a practice is the mechanism that ECOWAS practitioners use to acquire agency within the organization. By engaging in the practice of networking, practitioners are simultaneously agents within the organization and autonomous agents in the broader regional governance theatre.

ECOWAS practitioners use sensitization workshops to constitute themselves as agents within the organization and beyond. Sensitization workshops target key stakeholders and help direct the strategy and implementation of key organizational programs. For instance, in March 2020, the Vice President of the ECOWAS Commission, Madam Finda Koroma, organized a sensitization workshop toward the establishment of a National Early Warning and Response Centre in Accra, Ghana. Vice President Koroma in her remarks cited the need to build member state capacity to deal with the increasing human security threats. Similarly, in September 2016, the commission held a sensitization workshop for the Nigerian media on the impacts of the ECOWAS/EU Economic Partnership Agreement (EPA). The commission's role here was to build the knowledge of media practitioners around the tenets of the international trade agreement while simultaneously developing relationships between the organization and the media as a means to demonstrate ECOWAS' people-centric orientation.

The significance of networking as a practice and the constitution of practitioners as agents is that they enable practitioners to display their agency across scales of governance. As individuals, practitioners can tap into their understanding of how the organization works and use the practice of networking to make that understanding intelligible to those they interface with. Collectively, networking is part of the repertoire of practices that account for how organizational officials acquire agency. Most importantly, the outcomes of networking help fill uneven power vacuums within regional arrangements (Ohanyan 2014). This dynamic is apparent in the increasing impact of civil society organizations in the ECOWAS Court of Justice. From 2017 to 2020, civil society organizations in West Africa have successfully brought cases to the ECOWAS Court of Justice. The court has more often ruled in favor of civil society and against ECOWAS member states. In 2018, a civil society group, Law and Rights Awareness Initiative, brought a case against the Nigerian government, stating that the government had violated the right to freedom of expression with Section 24 of its Cybercrime Act of 2015. The ECOWAS Court ruled that the Nigerian government needed to amend the bill to align with Article 1 of the African Charter on Human and People's rights and the International Covenant on Civil and Political Rights. The Court also ruled against Togo's 2017 internet shutdown and ordered Guinea to pay over $47 million in compensation to a South African energy company for violation of its property rights. The networking between civil society actors and ECOWAS practitioners help create a regional context where stakeholders in the region can challenge the state-centric status quo of the organization, and civil society actors and other actors are enabled by their networked relations with practitioners across institutional contexts.

Organizational Dynamism as Practice

Just as networking is critical to the practitioners, their ability to engage in networking is supplemented by the institutional space created to do so, otherwise known as organizational dynamism. While one may suspect that ECOWAS practitioners are constrained by the preferences of the Authority Heads of State, it is the mandate and activities of practitioners that create the change permitting properties of the organization. The Authority Heads of State and Government would often render a decision at an ordinary session, charging the ECOWAS Commission to take up specific policies or strategies. This opening allows practitioners to implement or change existing institutional rules in new ways allowing us to observe forms of incremental change within an institutional analysis.[9]

The institutional space provided to practitioners illustrates what Mahoney and Thelen call a "power-distribution" view of institutions, emphasizing ongoing struggles within and over institutional arrangements. They argue, in part, that the cumulative effects of institutional power struggles allow institutions to not only survive, but also position to become significant political actors.[10] As power is (in)directly distributed to practitioners, they are able to acquire agency (through their autonomy) and have the capacity to implement incremental shifts to the ECOWAS.

ECOWAS's Sahel Policy offers an apt example of how institutional power is distributed to practitioners within ECOWAS. The Authority Heads of State and Government in July 2013 tasked the ECOWAS Commission to formulate an ECOWAS Sahel Strategy. From there, practitioners within the commission drafted a preliminary ECOWAS Sahel Strategy document that was used at an international consultative meeting in Washington, D.C., in October 2013. The consultative meeting was held at the margins of the annual meetings of the World Bank and the International Monetary Fund (IMF). This initial consultative meeting established the Coordination Platform that would be used to set up two sets of recurring meetings to take place in West Africa and in Washington, D.C., that would consist of ECOWAS member states, regional and international organizations such as Union Economique et Monetaire Ouest Africain/Economic and Monetary Union of West Africa (UEMOA), Permanent Interstate Committee for drought control in the Sahel (CILSS), and Authorite du liptako gourma/liptako gourma authority (ALG), and ECOWAS "partners." The Sahel Strategy aimed to develop a synergy of actions under a strengthened coordination mechanism, toward an effective implementation of Sahelian development. The ECOWAS Sahel Strategy outlined an action plan that strategized coordination in intervention, transport infrastructure, food security, and peace and security. The outcome of this strategy was the development of 31 major projects designed for implementation over 5 years, which would cost 4.75 billion USD.

Securing the Sahel is a frontline issue within ECOWAS, as the insurgents have threatened the peace and security of ECOWAS member states. The Sahel has also served as a strategic priority for countries focused on counterterrorism, such as the United States. The development and coordination of ECOWAS' strategy for this high-stake issue area that is left to the ECOWAS Commission is illuminating for a couple of reasons. First, it casts doubt on the idea that ECOWAS Heads of States are constraints to organizational progress. One version of this analysis could claim that the vague directive to "develop a strategy" limits the scope of what could be done due to ambiguity by the chief decision-makers of the organization. However, it is precisely this ambiguity that provides ECOWAS practitioners institutional space to interpret that directive using their own discretion and ideas. Organizational dynamism acknowledges the "gaps" or "soft spots" within an institution and considers the ways in which practitioners work within those areas to create institutional change and contributes to the durability of the organization.

Evolution of ECOWAS' Institutional Development

Democracy promotion has been a central feature of ECOWAS' institutional development, following the idea that the regime types within a given region must be mostly the same for deep processes of regionalization and region-building to occur (Kahler and Macintyre 2013; Kühnhardt 2010). Many practitioners refer ECOWAS as the most democratically developed sub-regional grouping in Africa, due to its institutionalization of democratic and good governance principles. The development of democracy in West Africa is meant to challenge the notion that West African states and ECOWAS as an organization have become less elite-centric, as progress in democratization elicits greater demands for openness and engagement with civilians in the region-building process. Under this assumption, democratization would enable convergence and agency among and between regional stakeholders.

In practice, the process of democratization in ECOWAS member states has varied significantly. Such democratization processes are often impeded by a multiplicity of actors, attitudes, and conflicts (Diamond 2008). The democratization process might also be limited by the existence of autocratic personal rulers, highly centralized and overpowering presidencies, and underdeveloped political institutions (Diamond 2008). Over the last 20 years, processes of democratization in Africa have produced areas of complexity and contestation such as illegitimate military intervention, the emergence of hybrid regimes, democratic institutionalization, and endemic corruption, among many others (Lynch and Crawford 2011). This pessimism around the process of democratization in West Africa makes ECOWAS's overt institutional commitment to democracy and good governance a puzzling feature of convergence and agency.

How does the process of democratization impact how (1) ECOWAS institutions evolve over time and (2) practitioners engage in the work of convergence and agency? ECOWAS has implemented four organizational changes that reflect the broader institutional evolution to focus more on political security, democracy, and good governance. It also provides a context in which practitioners draw their background institutional knowledge to facilitate convergence and agency. Embedded in each of these reforms is an overt declaration of ECOWAS' normative preference that its member states adhere to principles of democracy and good governance. This should be reflected in each member state's institutional makeup and be promoted as regional values of stability.

One of the first reforms toward a more democratically inclined ECOWAS was the Declaration of Political Principles in January 1991. The declaration acknowledges ECOWAS's recognition of a need to "intensify and strengthen their integration efforts" to achieve regional solidarity (ECOWAS 1991). ECOWAS' political principles stress that the organization will "promote and encourage the full enjoyment by all our peoples their fundamental human, political, economic, social and cultural rights." It also highlights ECOWAS's commitment and belief in liberty and "inalienable rights to participate through free and democratic processes" within member states. The Declaration of Political Principles is one of the first instances early in ECOWAS' existence where explicit values of democracy are outlined and promoted. The Declaration also emerges in the context of ECOWAS' presence in an ongoing civil conflict in Liberia and Sierra Leone, which also informed the organization's desire to promote peaceful democratic transitions in the declaration.

Perhaps one of the biggest indications of a normative shift in ECOWAS is its revised treaty in 1993. The revised treaty contains 93 Articles versus 65 in the original treaty and covers more areas such as migration, tourism, human resources, transfer of arms, and social capital, accounting for the political, security, and social issues in the region. An important area of expansion is in the various protocols amended to the revised treaty that supplement Article 58 (regional security). Article 76 and Article 77 give ECOWAS dispute resolution power and sanction power, both of which strengthen the decision and discretionary power of ECOWAS. These revisions to the treaty suggest that in order to match and potentially enforce democratic values in the region, expanding and revising the treaty would be necessary to develop the parameters that would facilitate and legitimate any institutional effort to converge toward democratic governance.

Further institutionalizing the convergence toward democratic governance was the Protocol relating to the Mechanism for Conflict Prevention, Management, Resolution Peace-keeping and Security in 1999. Known simply as "The Mechanism," the protocol aims to strengthen, consolidate, and maintain peace and security in West Africa by applying the protocol in any instances of internal conflict, violations of human rights, aggression between member states, an overthrow or attempted overthrow of democratically elected governments, or at the discretion of the Mechanism's Mediation and Security Council (Article 25).[11]

The Mechanism is supplemented by the Protocol on Democracy and Good Governance in 2001, which stipulates that all member states should have a separation of power between the executive, judicial, and legislative branches of government. The supplementary protocol also suggests that any West African leader ought to ascend to power through free, fair, and transparent elections, while asserting a zero tolerance for power obtained or maintained by unconstitutional means. Article 1 also stresses the preference for popular decision-making and "strict adherence to democratic principles and decentralization of power at all levels of government." The protocol also establishes the role of the armed forces and security forces in a democracy, stressing the importance of nonpartisanship, authority vested under legal civilians, and loyalty to the nation. Member states are also required to provide a venue to alleviate poverty, promote basic human needs for their population, and exchange students and academics, culture, and religion.

Section VII defines rule of law as "not only good laws that are in conformity with the provision on human rights, but also a good judicial system, a good system of administration, and good management of the State apparatus" (Article 33 (1)). Section VIII emphasizes the important role for women and children in consolidating a democratic region, stipulating that member states need to guarantee children's rights and give them access to education. The protocol puts the onus of implementation on member states and threatens the use of sanctions, ECOWAS suspension, and the refusal to support candidates presented by the member state concerned for elective posts in international organizations (Article 45) if states do not abide by the contents of the protocol.

ECOWAS' institutional changes represent an attempt by the organization to create a regional environment premised on democracy and good governance, one that can hold states and subversive leaders accountable for undemocratic acts. Thus, there is a conscious attempt by ECOWAS to pair the process of democratization within member states with regional institutional reforms that align with democratic reforms in member states. Despite these early institutional reforms, there has been mixed results of the practice and process of democratization across West Africa. What motivates practitioners in ECOWAS to continue to pursue principles of democracy and good governance where member state compliance is unlikely? The conceptual framework provided in this chapter seeks to uncover how practitioners use their agency to pursue institutional reforms while creating networks to create bottom-up relationships with civil society to drive democratic change within member states. Through these institutional reforms, we begin to see a shift in the normative foundations of the organization.

Conclusion

This chapter develops a framework to examine region-building by focusing on understanding the factors and interaction patterns that drive institutional change in ECOWAS. This chapter offers a way to look at the process in which practitioners in ECOWAS rely on their background knowledge and activism as autonomous international bureaucrats to create the conditions for convergence in the region. Another important role of this chapter is to show that region-building in West Africa is dynamic—a process that arises and evolves over time. The emphasis is placed on the drivers of region-building to examine regionalism in West Africa and Africa more broadly beyond whether it is "effective" or if it "works." By emphasizing practitioners as the drivers of region-building in West Africa, this framework offers a narrative on region-building that places a scope on the degrees of interaction among actors that allows for new patterns and forms of regionalism to emerge. The framework presented here accentuates the need to examine and highlight experiences, interaction, and features within ECOWAS that drive actors toward a common conception of the region's role in governance. As the comparative regionalism literature has called for increased attention to identity-laden and social context variables, the conceptual framework presented in this chapter brings together the concepts of practice, the tenets of Pan-Africanism, and networked governance as highly interactive properties that comprise the building of a practical, inclusive, and connected West Africa, with ECOWAS as the conduit.

In the chapters that follow, I highlight how regional convergence in West Africa takes two paths. First, I will highlight the organizational dynamism and evolution in ECOWAS, from an organization built to deal in areas of economic integration, to an organization with political and security mandates, and to the organization that it is today that minimizes the role of the heads of states and is embedded in the social areas of West African life. The second path to convergence emphasizes the specified regional activities that represent networked region-building and the emergent properties of regional convergence in ECOWAS.

Notes

1 Regionalism, broadly understood, often refers to formal, state-led projects and processes and a body of norms, values, objectives, ideas, and a type of regional order (Schulz et al. 2001; Wunderlich 2007). Regionalization, broadly understood, is an empirical trend depicting a multidimensional process of intra-regional change that occurs simultaneously at several levels of social, political, and economic interactions (Hettne 1999). These definitions are highly contested, and much of the comparative regionalism literature argues that the concepts of regionalism and regionalization are context specific. One might also conflate region-building, regionalism, regionalization with regional integration, which, broadly understood, is the process in which states come together to achieve goals of peace and security or economic harmonization.

2 The philosophical, cultural, and social promotion of Afro-centrism, manifested through Maafa studies (study of African enslavement), calls for Africans on the continent and in the diaspora to recognize hundreds of years of suffering and to embrace the development of a historical narrative of Africa premised on African agency and less so on depictions of Africa that derive from the West.

3 Mumford, Densua (2021). “How Regional Norms Shape Regional Organizations: The Pan-African Rhetorical Trap and the Empowerment of the ECOWAS Parliament.” *African Affairs*, adaa033, https://doi.org/10.1093/afraf/adaa033.

4 Fanta (2008) argues that shadow regionalism manifests itself as a component of African regionalism because of the parallel existence of neopatrimonialism at the regional level. Shadow regionalism refers to:

> A situation where two somewhat parallel structure of power exists in regard to the regional integration process. One is the formal process marked by the regional organizations and agreements reached at the regional level, while the second process concerns the informal links that are established among the many actors interacting within the region—African states adopt a dual strategy. One refers to the official stance and is in line with the regional or international regulations. The second one is not officially recognized but still better allows the state leaders to achieve some of their aims. The unofficial support that states provide to insurgents in a neighboring country offers a very good example also because it is widespread and is a historical phenomenon in Africa.

5 For example, in Asian regionalism, Katzenstein (1997, 3) focuses on the impact of informal interactions by highlighting the inclusive character of Asia's market-driven integration and contrasts with the exclusive character of Europe's formal institutions—he argues that private keiretsu networks worked with the Japanese government and Chinese networks to substitute for rule-based regional institutions, explaining the causal power of these networks through norms and domestic state structures. Informality in the Asian context is viewed as more legitimate than informality in the African context; however, it is worth probing the similarities.

6 See Shaw (2003) and Rittberger and Nettesheim (2008) for commentary on the emergence of new issue areas relative to the uneven impact of globalization.

7 I use language from Checkel (2015, 563) to highlight how my perspective to region-building answers his call on how to measure and account for the empirical role of ideas and identity in comparative regionalism.

8 Region-building in West Africa (and Africa more broadly) has been bound to ideas such as regime-boosting, defined by Söderbaum as a "vivid game of rhetorical and symbolic regionalism, without implementation," and shadow regionalism, a façade of formal regionalism and diplomacy that is driven by bureaucrats from the state working with illegal businesspeople in order to bolster patronage networks and weaken political challengers or serve as instruments for self-enrichment.

9 Mahoney, James and Kathleen Thelen (2010). Explaining Institutional Change: Ambiguity, Agency, and Power. Cambridge: Cambridge University Press.

10 Ibid, page 2.

11 A more complete discussion of the contours of the mechanism appears in Chapter 3.

Bibliography

Adler-Nissen, Rebecca, and Alena Drieschova. 2019. "Track-Change Diplomacy: Technology, Affordances, and the Practice of International Negotiations." International Studies Quarterly 63(3): 531–545.

Adler, Emanuel, and Vincent Pouliot. 2011. International Practices. Cambridge University Press.

Bach, Daniel. 1995. "Francophone Regionalism or Franco-African Regionalism." In State and Society in Francophone Africa since Independence, eds. Anthony Kirk-Greene and Daniel Bach. London: Palgrave Macmillan, 200–212. https://link.springer.com/chapter/10.1007/978-1-349-23826-2_13.

Best, Jacqueline, and Alexandra Gheciu. 2014. The Return of the Public in Global Governance. London: Cambridge University Press.

Bueger, Christian. 2017. "Security as Practice." In Routledge Handbook of Security Studies, eds. Myriam Dunn Cavelty and Thierry Balzacq. New York: Routledge, 126–135.

———. 2019. "Performing Piracy: A Note on the Multiplicity of Agency." Journal of International Relations and Development 22(4): 832–852.

Clapham, Christopher. 1996. Africa and the International System. Cambridge: Cambridge University Press.

Diamond, Larry Jay. 2008. "The Rule of Law versus the Big Man." Journal of Democracy 19(2): 138–149. http://muse.jhu.edu/content/crossref/journals/journal_of_democracy/v019/19.2diamond.html (February 24, 2014).

Dingwerth, Klaus, and Philipp Pattberg. 2006. "Global Governance as a Perspective on World Politics." Global Governance: A Review of Multilateralism and International Organizations 12(2): 185–203.
Fanta, Emmanuel. 2008. Dynamics of Regional (Non-)Integration in Eastern Africa. http://cris.unu.edu/sites/cris.unu.edu/files/W-2008-2.pdf.
Fioramonti, Lorenzo, and Frank Mattheis. 2016. "Is Africa really following Europe? An integrated framework for comparative regionalism." JCMS: Journal of Common Market Studies 54(3): 674–690.
Glas, Aarie. 2018. "African Union Security Culture in Practice: African Problems and African Solutions." International Affairs 94(5): 1121–1138.
Glas, Aarie, and Emmanuel Balogun. 2020. "Norms in Practice: People-Centric Governance in ASEAN and ECOWAS." International Affairs 96(4): 1015–1032.
Hettne, Björn. 1999. Globalism and the New Regionalism. London: Palgrave Macmillan, 1–24.
Iheduru, Okechukwu. 2011. "The 'New' ECOWAS Implications for the Study of Regional Integration." In Ashgate Research Companion to Regionalisms, eds. Timothy M. Shaw, J. Andrew Grant, and Scarlett Cornelissen. Burlington: Ashgate, 213–241.
Isah, Abdulrasheed. 2018. "On Policy Reluctance and Economic Peril: Nigeria and the AfCFTA." *The Republic*, 2018. https://republic.com.ng/december-18-january-19/nigeria-afcfta/
Kahler, Miles, and Andrew Macintyre. 2013. Integrating Regions: Asia in Comparative Context. Stanford: Stanford University Press.
Katzenstein, Peter J. 2005. A World of Regions: Asia and Europe in the American Imperium. Ithaca: Cornell University Press.
Kühnhardt, Ludger. 2010. Region Building: Volume I: The Global Proliferation of Regional Integration. New York: Berghahn Books.
Lynch, Gabrielle, and Gordon Crawford. 2011. "Democratization in Africa 1990–2010: An Assessment." Democratization 18(2): 275–310. www.tandfonline.com/doi/abs/10.1080/13510347.2011.554175 (April 14, 2013).
Mansfield, Edward D, and Etel Solingen. 2010. "Regionalism." Annual Review of Political Science 13: 145–163.
Moravcsik, A. 1998. The Choice for Europe. Social Purpose and State Power from Messina to Maastricht. Cornell: Cornell University Press.
Moravcsik, Andrew, and Frank Schimmelfennig. 2009. "Liberal Intergovernmentalism." In European Integration Theory, 64–84. Oxford: Oxford University Press.
Ohanyan, Anna. 2014. Networked Regionalism as Conflict Management. Stanford: Stanford University Press.
Reno, William. 1995. Corruption and State Politics in Sierra Leone. Cambridge: Cambridge University Press.
Rosenau, James N. 2002. "Governance in a New Global Order." In Governing Globalization: Power, Authority, and Global Governance, eds. Anthony McGrew and David Held. Malden: Polity Press.
Schulz, Michael, Fredrik Söderbaum, and Joakim Ojendal. 2001. Regionalization in a Globalizing World. London: Zed Books. London
Söderbaum, Fredrik, and Ian Taylor, eds. 2008. Afro-Regions: The Dynamics of Cross-Border Micro-Regionalism in Africa. Stockholm: Nordiska Afrikainstituet.

Solingen, Etel. 2008. "The Genesis, Design and Effects of Regional Institutions: Lessons from East Asia and the Middle East." International Studies Quarterly 52(2): 261–294. http://doi.wiley.com/10.1111/j.1468-2478.2008.00501.x.

Tieku, Thomas Kwesi. 2017. Governing Africa: 3D Analysis of the African Union's Performance. Lanham: Rowman & Littlefield.

Van Langenhove, Luk, and Philippe De Lombaerde. 2007. "Regional Integration Poverty and Social Policy." Global Social Policy 7(3): 379–385.

Wunderlich, Jens-Uwe. 2007. Regionalism, Globalization and International Order. Ashgate Publishing Company.

Young, Crawford. 2012. The Postcolonial State in Africa: Fifty Years of Independence, 1960–2010. Madison: University of Wisconsin Press.

3 Convergence and Agency in Peace and Security

The presidential elections in The Gambia in December of 2016 were part of a wave of democratic elections across West Africa. Cabo Verde, Niger, Benin, Chad, and Ghana were holding presidential elections in 2016. Despite the presence of recycled elites in some elections such as in Niger and Chad, observers of West African elections were relatively optimistic about the prospect for democracy in West Africa.[1] These elections would represent the first time since the creation of Economic Community of West African States (ECOWAS) all member states that were at least nominally elected, a sign of West Africa's incremental progress toward a democratic region.

However, the political context in The Gambia represented a different reality. There was no political transition in power through elections in the 50 years since independence and the then president Yahya Jammeh had been in power (via coup) since 1994. Jammeh made many public declarations on his intention to be president for life. Under Jammeh's rule, The Gambia received plenty of scrutiny from international human rights organizations such as Amnesty International and Human Rights Watch for Jammeh's treatment and torture of journalists and activists and for Jammeh's refusal to register international election observers in the country.

Despite this reality, Gambians went to the polls early December 2016 and ousted Jammeh. Opposition candidate Adam Barrow won just over 43% of the vote. Initially, Jammeh conceded victory to Barrow, did not express contempt with the vote, and vowed not to contest the results. A week later, Jammeh came out and questioned the legitimacy of the electoral process and called for new elections, and in following days, Jammeh deployed Gambian troops to the capital city of Banjul and troops seized control of the Electoral Commission, causing Barrow to flee to Senegal, raising the likelihood of popular unrest.

Jammeh's defiance and the other events surrounding the election of Adam Barrow prompted regional attention, as ECOWAS, the African Union (AU), the UN, and the United States condemned Jammeh's rejection of the results. Further, the AU and the United Nations (UN) in particular agreed to consider and uphold the subsidiarity principle and left ECOWAS to consider intervention into The Gambia in order to uphold the election results and

DOI: 10.4324/9780429436734-3

remove Jammeh from power. While ECOWAS Heads of States from Senegal, Ghana, Nigeria, and Liberia had a hard time convincing Jammeh to accept the election results and were considering their options regarding intervention, Barrow was sworn into the presidency on January 19, 2017 and the UN Security Council passed Resolution 2337, which recognized Barrow as the president of The Gambia and backed ECOWAS' efforts to remove Jammeh from power. Part of the organization's effort to remove Jammeh came through the ECOWAS Mission to The Gambia, (ECOMIG) also known as "Operation Restore Democracy" to ensure that Jammeh would not interrupt the transfer of power. ECOMIG consisted of over 7,000 ECOWAS troops that surrounded The Gambia by land, sea, and air, to ensure that The Gambia did not destabilize under Jammeh's defiance. At the end of it all, Jammeh reluctantly fled The Gambia, without ECOWAS having to remove Jammeh from the country forcibly. However, the newly installed President Barrow requested that ECOWAS troops remain in The Gambia to ensure peace and security.

Elsewhere in the region, Guinean President Alpha Conde, who rose to power in December 2010 as the first democratically elected leader in the country's history, attempted to change the Guinean constitution to extend term limits and stay in power for a third term in October 2020. Despite extensive resistance from civil society and political opposition parties in Guinea, Conde won a third term and ECOWAS and other external observers deemed that the election was conducted credibly and legitimately.

Through what some have coined "coercive diplomacy," the removal of Jammeh is an illustration of a trend in ECOWAS' development of democracy and good governance (Ateku 2020). However, the example of Conde's attempt to extend his presidential term represents a familiar story of executives in West Africa attempting to rig institutional rules to preserve power. This chapter examines the institutional development of democracy and good governance in ECOWAS, through the vantage point of peace and security. The chapter also examines how early arguments and institutional innovations around peace and security issues created the institutional space and background conditions for practitioners to articulate and create meanings of democracy and good governance in West Africa. The chapter examines ECOWAS' institutional development as it pertains to peace and security, particularly how the organization can use military intervention and institutional mechanisms, such as the Protocol of Democracy and Good Governance Supplemental Protocol for Democracy and Good Governance (also known as "the Mechanism") and the ECOWAS Conflict Prevention Framework (ECPF) to develop locally cultivated networks in peace and security, that are also inclusive of non-state regional stakeholders. Taken together, these protocols serve as tools to promote democracy and good governance in West Africa.

This chapter is motivated by two empirical puzzles and a broader conceptual puzzle. The first empirical puzzle is the conventional discussion regarding the norm of noninterference/unconstitutional changes in government in Africa (sometimes referred to as the "anti-coup" norm), which is tethered to the idea that these events happened spontaneously or selectively (Bareebe 2018). Matters of regime change are typically considered areas of domestic concern. However, the OAU/AU have frequently opted for the "Hear no evil, see no evil, speak no evil" doctrine, condoning a "culture of impunity." This conventional view not only leaves out the important role of early warning, election monitoring, public opinion, and civil society activism and mobilization in cultivating the relevant information about possible regime change, but also does not consider the process in which "coercive diplomacy" becomes a part of the repertoire of ECOWAS in its ability and desire to respond to issues of democracy and good governance. Additionally, there are arguments that ECOWAS takes political crises "case by case"—instead, this chapter emphasizes how issues of peace and security/democracy and good governance become crucial as normative standards of practice within the region and the role practitioners plan in deepening these practices in the region (Odigie 2019; Hartmann 2017; Kaboré 2018).

The second puzzle addresses the central themes of the book, which raises questions on the enduring role of the Authority Heads of States in ECOWAS, and their centrality in facilitating democracy and good governance. Instead of focusing on the Heads of States' performance, this chapter considers the activist role of ECOWAS practitioners in discerning the feasibility and capability of ECOWAS intervention, with their activities over time solidifying and legitimating ECOWAS' mandate.

The chapter examines regional responses to unconstitutional changes in the government and the like not as episodic moments, but as moments that represent attempts to deepen the organizational commitments to democracy, good governance, peace, and security. Returning to the illustration of the "Gambian moment," for example, we ought not to look at it as a moment that signifies a turning point for ECOWAS and its stance on unconstitutional changes in government; instead, the chapter hones in on how ECOWAS practitioners, through their day-to-day practices and interactions with an assortment of regional stakeholders, make the path to a more democratic region, intelligible. Using the lens of regional convergence, we can examine the socialization of actors and processes within ECOWAS, particularly the relationship between agency, material, and natural environments.

The chapter proceeds in four parts. First is an examination of the founding arguments of ECOWAS and early interactions between member states regarding democracy and good governance. Examining these early arguments provides insight into how ECOWAS dealt with questions of regional stability and how the responses to these questions of regional stability end up conditioning the region to the practice of intervention. This section also examines the development of institutional mechanisms that permit ECOWAS to use intervention as a tool to reconcile regional instability and provides a context for understanding ECOWAS' initial ideas surrounding noninterference.

The next section explores two ECOWAS transformations: the first in 1993 with the revision of the original treaty of Lagos and the second with the creation of the ECOWAS Commission in 2007. This section also traces the associated institutional measures promoting democracy and good governance, specifically the protocols that precede the ECOWAS Revised Treaty to understand ECOWAS' approaches to peace, absent the integration of civil society stakeholders. The section also examines the institutionalization of democracy and good governance through the Protocol Relating to the Mechanism for Conflict Prevention (1999) and the Supplementary Protocol of Democracy and Good Governance (2001) in the first transformation and the creation of the ECOWAS (ECPF) in the second transformation, creating the institutional space for ECOWAS practitioners to deepen the progress toward democracy and good governance in the region.

The next section shows how ECOWAS practitioners work to incorporate regional stakeholders into the development of democracy and good governance, specifically highlighting various Ecocrat activities such as the collaboration between the West African Networking for Peacebuilding (WANEP) and the ECOWAS Early Warning Directorate, Ecocrat networking in election monitoring, ECOWAS Commission and foreign policy relationships, and the incorporation of humanitarian law practices into the ECOWAS Standby Force (ESF). The chapter concludes by addressing the implications of the emergence of ECOWAS practitioners as relevant actors in promoting and deepening democracy and good governance in West Africa.

Founding Conditions of ECOWAS: Contrasting Notions of Noninterference

In the years leading up to and immediately following the creation of ECOWAS, it was common to see West African leaders who were critical of each other regarding the political development of the region and the constituent member states. For example, as indicated in the previous chapter, one of the main contentions at the organization's founding was Cote d' Ivoire's support of Biafra during the Nigerian Civil War. West African heads of states often held the understanding that commenting on the affairs of neighboring states is expected among each other, while in their external dealings in the OAU and other international settings, West African states adhered to principles of noninterference into the internal affairs of states. The contrasting notion of noninterference typically characterized African leaders as "indifferent" to notions of accountability in instances of human rights violations and democratic governance. However, the posturing and positioning of West African state interference is and has been permissible as a normalized practice in the region. Thus, in this context, we can define and understand interference in West Africa in the following ways. First, interference can be understood as the sovereign equality of states that privileges group unity or harmony, which renders the mere commenting about or criticizing the affairs of member states unacceptable in any circumstance (Klein 1974). Interference can also be defined and understood as the performance of publicly entering into another country given a specific political and social context. Thus, noninterference should be considered a defense mechanism for African states' relations external to the content, mediated by notions and legacies of Pan-African solidarity. In West Africa, interference became a habit of intraregional relations, due to the shared consciousness of Pan-African solidarity and the background ideas that African leaders could get their affairs in order by holding themselves accountable and simply because there were many issues and conflicts for West African leaders to comment on.

Understanding this context of West African leaders commenting on each other, yet coordinating in solidarity on the international stage is important to the regional development of democracy and good governance for two main reasons. The first reason is that it gives us insight into how leaders at the outset of the organization would consider issues of consensus, decision-making, and relationship-building and the extent to which the organization would be used as a tool to build consensus among actors. The second reason is that it focuses on how regional contexts may serve as an opportunity structure for negotiating and creating resonance for democracy and good governance practices. What follows is a discussion of ECOWAS's institutional moves immediately following the creation of the organization to show how the founding conditions of intraregional argumentation informed particular organizational decisions around democracy and good governance.

Democracy and Good Governance: Pre-Liberia

In April of 1978, ECOWAS passed its first institutional protocol, the Protocol on Non-Aggression. The protocol was relevant and necessary as member states such as Nigeria experienced back-to-back military coups in 1976 and 1977. The protocol confirmed the inherent skepticism from the Anglophone ECOWAS states and the CEAO (Economic Community of West African States) member states, who believed that even though they were part of ECOWAS, the organization still posed a threat to the existence and survival of CEAO. For instance, CEAO states advocated for the following article (Article 2) to be added to the protocol:

> Each Member State shall refrain, from committing, encouraging or condoning acts of subversion, hostility or aggression against the territorial integrity or political independence of the other Member States.[2]

Other articles in the protocol specify "foreigners" both "resident and non-Resident" from being "aggressive" toward other ECOWAS members. There are multiple meanings implied with this language. First, the use of "aggression" refers to the supposition that states within ECOWAS could influence the politics and subvert a regional rival through external forces—and commenting on the affairs of other member states could also serve as a form of "aggression."

The reference to resident and nonresident foreigners meant both actors external to the region, state-to-state conflict, and individuals who travel from their home country to be a hostile actor in another ECOWAS state.

The protocol served partially as a safeguard to prevent conflict among members in the new organization, while also responding to the persistence of domestic instability within member states. The Non-Aggression protocol was also symbolic. It was an immediate institutional response to a series of military coups in one of its founding members, indicating a consciousness of the organization's responsibility to maintain peace and security.

Shortly after establishing the Non-Aggression protocol, ECOWAS passed the Protocol Relating to Mutual Assistance on Defense (A/SP3/5/81) in 1981. This protocol goes further than the Non-Aggression protocol. It states that any threat against a member state in ECOWAS is a threat against the whole region (Article 2) and that member states resolve to provide "mutual aid" to any member state that is under the threat of aggression (Article 3).

The Mutual Assistance Protocol is a significant institutional development for two main reasons. First is that it establishes "rules of engagement" by ECOWAS in the instance of inter- and intrastate conflict. Whereas the Non-Aggression protocol sought to protect the territorial integrity of states and stipulates that ECOWAS members should not move to infringe on each other's right to political independence, the Mutual Assistance protocol sought to mobilize the whole region in response to any inherent or immediate threats to or within a member state. Concerning the rules of engagement, Article 4 in the protocol states:

> Member States shall also take appropriate measures such as specified in Articles 17 and 18 of the present Protocol in the following circumstances:
> (a) In case of armed conflict between two or several member states if the settlement procedure by peaceful means as indicated in Article 5 of the Non-Aggression Protocol mentioned in the Preamble proves ineffective.
> (b) In case of internal armed conflict within any Member State engineered and supported actively from outside likely to endanger the security and peace in the entire Community. In this case the Authority shall appreciate and decide on this situation in full collaboration with the Authority of the Member State or state or state concerned.

The second reason is that the Mutual Defense protocol is the first attempt at institutionalizing and articulating the practice of interference by ECOWAS in a member state. As Article 4 indicates, the Mutual Assistance protocol does not merely assert that member states are only responsible for the peace and security in the threat of interstate conflict, but it also explicitly mentions mutual assistance for *internal* armed conflicts that actors outside of the region support. Again, the language is purposeful. Determining on what grounds ECOWAS can justify its means of intervention in internal conflicts, particularly in using the phrase "engineered and supported actively from outside" and "likely to endanger the security and peace in the entire community," allows for variable interpretation of what external or engineered support would look like in the region and to define what constitutes as aggression. The perambulatory clauses in the protocol also stipulate that foreign military bases in West African countries are considered threats or external aggression. So long as a member state could prove or frame a narrative that internal aggression toward its state is derived from an external actor, ECOWAS would have the ability to intervene on the behalf of that member state. Article 18 of the Mutual Assistance protocol states this plainly:

1. In the case where an internal conflict in a Member State of the Community is actively maintained and sustained from outside, the provisions of Articles 6, 9 and 16 of this Protocol shall apply.
2. Community forces shall not intervene if the conflict remains purely internal.

Article 18 still considers the question of subversion and territorial integrity. Including "purely internal" would refer to domestic crises such as civil conflict or potentially unlawful political transitions. Article 18 would also allow a West African leader to consider a civil conflict purely internally driven to keep other states from interfering in the conflict. Conversely, if a rebel group attempted to subvert a member state and organized this effort external to the state, it gave ECOWAS permission to intervene.

The Mutual Assistance protocol signified a desire among ECOWAS members to create provisions within the organizations that would also carry with them some normative values and move its governance ideas into practice. Instrumentally, Mutual Assistance Protocol relied on coordination between the Authority Heads of State and a newly created Defense Council and Defense Commission. The Authority Heads of state would decide on the necessity of military intervention in the instance of conflict and would deploy a standing military unit, called the Allied Armed Forces of the Community (AAFC). The AAFC would be a contingent of military officials from member states, led by a force commander, typically a senior serving military officer in a member state (Articles 12 and 13). The Defense Council would consist of Ministers of Defense and Foreign Affairs in member states (Article 7), with the possibility of expansion given the severity of the conflict. The Defense Council was also responsible for threat assessment and for developing a strategy in the instance of intervention. The Defense Commission would consist of a "chief of staff" from each member state charged with examining the technical capacity of defense matters in the instance of intervention (Article 11). In instances where ECOWAS would determine a state or an actor to be an aggressor in a conflict, ECOWAS would consider any existing defense agreement to be invalid—thus, the ECOWAS mandate would supersede any bilateral arrangement that would protect an aggressive party (Article 20).

After establishing the Mutual Assistance protocol, the commentary stressed its significance as the perception was that African countries as they moved further away from their colonial legacies would be more vulnerable to external aggression. However, the limit of the protocol was the lack of capacity to implement some of its critical institutional components. Primarily, the lack of an actual standing army (AAFC would be a contingent of earmarked troops from each member state), and inability to deploy the standing army if it did exist, proved to be key operational limitations to realizing the potential of the protocol.

The Mutual Assistance protocol does have significance toward the institutional development of ECOWAS down the road. First, the protocol reveals that there was a collective concern about internal and external hostility among and within member states and provided at the very least the parameters and ideas around intraregional solidarity. Second, the protocol highlights ECOWAS member state perceptions that it was necessary to create a way for the organization and its members to intervene should regional threats emerge, but that the right to intervention should be embedded in the organization's practices. Third and related, the protocol credits ECOWAS's fluid institutional design, exemplified by the desire to create the Defense Council and Defense Commission. The Mutual Assistance protocol indicated the scope of the distributional issues at the core of the organization. The need to enforce a Mutual Assistance protocol by creating new institutional bodies stems from both the politically contested nature of ECOWAS' institutional rules and a degree of openness in the interpretation and implementation of these rules. Even when institutions are formally codified, their guiding expectations often remain ambiguous and are subject to interpretation, debate, and contestation.

The Mutual Aggression protocol and the Non-Aggression protocol set a precedent in the organization, particularly in that it begins an articulation of how ECOWAS begins to think about security broadly and how the organization should consider the internal dynamics of its members. The Protocols of Non-Aggression and Mutual Defense had both practical and normative significance for the development of ECOWAS. They made clear the commitment to an ECOWAS-led preservation of peace and security. More importantly, they signified that ECOWAS would consider collective intervention as a practice in the subregion. However, the protocols lacked a tether to the domestic political structures of member states and relied on member states to request ECOWAS assistance for the protocols to hold. As a result, it would take nine years after creating the Mutual Assistance protocol to test whether ECOWAS's normative commitment to regional security could materialize in practice.

Institutional Evolution: From ECOMOG to ECPF

The next phase in ECOWAS' institutional evolution in peace and security is the creation and operationalization of ECOWAS Ceasefire Monitoring Group (ECOMOG). In December 1989, Charles Taylor and his rebel forces, the National Patriotic Front of Liberia (NPFL) invaded Liberia and launched a brutal civil war. ECOWAS had initially declared the conflict in Liberia as "purely internal," and it took seven months after the conflict commenced for ECOWAS to convene and discuss a possible intervention into the conflict. Nigerian President Ibrahim Babangida commented on the breakdown in society, the loss of credibility, and the inability to govern as a means to justify an intervention into Liberia.[3] At an ECOWAS summit in June of 1990 in Banjul, The Gambia, ECOWAS member states were informed of sub-state actors providing funds and small arms to both sides of the conflict. As a result, a Standing Mediation Committee (SMC) was established, represented by Nigeria, Ghana, The Gambia, Sierra Leone, and Togo. The SMC convened an extraordinary session in Bamako, Mali in November 1990 to establish ECOMOG to oversee a peace plan signed by all warring factions. The SMC invoked Article 6(4) of the Mutual Assistance protocol, which makes any decision made by the Authority Heads of States enforceable by all member states. There was no need for full consensus by all member states, which caused most of the Francophone states in ECOWAS to pause in their support for a Liberian intervention. With the exception of Togo, there were no Francophone states that were party to the development of ECOMOG. Félix Houphouët-Boigny, the President of Côte d'Ivoire, also accused Nigeria and the SMC, for protracting the conflict, given that the organization was not invited by Liberian President Samuel Doe, nor was the intervention sanctioned by the UN.

The intention of ECOMOG was to be the main entity for mediation between Taylor and the NPFL and Samuel Doe. The use of ECOMOG was the first instance in post-colonial Africa that there was an organic, African-created mediation unit to intervene in a civil conflict. The SMC, directly after creating ECOMOG, pushed for elections and the creation of an interim government in Liberia, which ECOWAS would monitor. ECOMOG was intended to be a collective mechanism to restore governance in Liberia, providing a "homegrown" solution to what was an already brutal conflict. Despite the effort by the organization, ECOMOG was also widely considered an institutional failure due to ECOWAS' inability to support the mission of ECOMOG with proper organizational, administrative, and peacekeeping resources. Particularly, the inability to deploy a standing army in accordance with the Mutual Assistance protocol and representative of all ECOWAS member states limited the scope of ECOWAS' intervention. According to initial communiques establishing ECOMOG, Nigeria, Ghana, Guinea, and The Gambia were the only countries to contribute troops to the initial ECOMOG mission. In addition to the limited capacity of ECOMOG, parties to the conflict, such as Charles Taylor, did not view ECOMOG as legitimate enough to take seriously, as he did not attend either of the first two ECOMOG-led peace talks, Banjul I and Banjul II. Perhaps the factor that contributed the most to ECOMOG's limited capacity was that the organization was divided on the mission and the appropriateness of ECOWAS' presence in the conflict. Côte d'Ivorie and Burkina Faso were strong opponents to intervention. Generally, the Francophone member states took the perspective that ECOMOG intervention was a collective spectacle that "looked like a rescue mission" for Samuel Doe. Member states that were still a part of the CEAO stressed their frustrations about the lack of consultation afforded to Francophone states during the decision-making process for intervention (Adebajo 2002).

Beyond the operational hurdles, the success and struggles of ECOMOG reveal important continuities in the behaviors of member states. ECOMOG highlighted a seemingly inherent struggle among and between member states to build trust and standards for equal commitment and contribution. This struggle made it necessary for ECOWAS members to focus its institutional prerogatives on creating conditions in which all member states felt that they could commit to a collective mission of ECOWAS and build the institutional mechanisms that induce inclusive consensus among its member states and later, other regional stakeholders. ECOWAS attempted to address the need for inclusivity by creating the "Committee of Five," a group of mostly Francophone ECOWAS member states that would become more active in the negotiating and peace processes in the Liberian Civil War. The Committee of Five consisted of Cote d'Ivoire, Senegal, Togo, Guinea-Bissau, and The Gambia, and this group would lead ECOMOG negotiations with Amos Sawyer, the head of the interim Government, and Charles Taylor in 1991 during the Yamoussoukro Accords.

The emphasis on the development and events of the ECOMOG negotiations highlights both the contested relations between ECOWAS member states during one of its key institutional changes and how a process of argumentation and consensus-building often accompanies these institutional changes among members. This dynamic of institutional change and member state consensus building and/or disagreement is consistent with the organization's development. A clear example of this dynamic of consensus building is the progression of the ECOMOG negotiations. Three sets of negotiations in Banjul I, Banjul II (1990), and Lomé (1991) were products of the Anglophone-led SMC, while the Yamoussoukro Accords (1991) were the first negotiations led by the Committee of Five. The Yamoussoukro Accords are significant in that they were the first negotiations that would bring Charles Taylor and Amos Sawyer to negotiate a peace. The Yamoussoukro Accords also brought in external actors to the region, particularly the International Negotiation Network (INN)-led by former United States President Jimmy Carter to facilitate the electoral process in Liberia and the Committee of Five. The negotiations emphasized ECOWAS' desire to consolidate Liberia, a necessary atmosphere to conduct free, fair, and democratic elections, and to embed ECOMOG troops in designated areas throughout Liberia to facilitate the disarmament process on both sides of the conflict.

The content of these negotiations, which focused on creating democratic institutions and cessation of violence, would serve as the basis for ECOWAS to build its capacity to intervene over time. More importantly, the infusion of the CEAO states in the negotiation process helped improve the capacity of the ECOMOG mission. Further, the conscious inclusion of the INN by the Committee of Five helped legitimate the ECOMOG mandate among international observers. By the end of the Yamoussoukro Accords in October 1991, ECOMOG covered all of Liberia with election monitors and troops to supervise the encampment and disarmament of all warring factions in Liberia. The warring parties agreed to ECOMOG's presence in Liberia and afforded ECOWAS' neutrality in the war. ECOMOG would also monitor all entry points into Liberia. While the conflict in Liberia lasted until 2005 and ran concurrent to civil conflicts in Sierra Leone and Guinea-Bissau, the appropriateness and the capacity for ECOWAS to intervene in the civil disputes of its member states were instrumental in subsequent institutional innovations in organization, including a fundamental transformation in the focus of the organization.

ECOWAS' First Transformation: The Revised Treaty (1993–2007)

The ECOMOG experience also raised bigger questions about the organization's overall objective, the decision-making structure, and the struggles of building consensus among members. However, there were disagreements over how to make ECOMOG more effective on the ground and the role the organization should play in future instances of conflict resolution. There were also enduring questions of whether ECOWAS should continue down this path of interference, brought to bear the question of how to strengthen ECOWAS as an institution and embrace the differences among its actors.

ECOWAS's direction was first addressed during the 14th session of the Authority Heads of State from July 4–6, 1991, during the negotiations of the penultimate Yamoussoukro Accord. ECOWAS released what it would call the Declaration of Political Principles of ECOWAS (A/DCL.1/791). The Declaration of Political Principles laid out the organizations' commitment to the creation of a "stable and secure" political environment, free from threat of security, a consciousness of the rapidly changing international political landscape, and a renewed determination among the member states to consult each other more regularly and committing to harmonization and adoption of common policies and international negotiating positions. The Declaration of Political Principles and the session in general struck a tone of a need for an institutional "reset" of sorts—heads of states stressed during the summit the need to "speak as one ECOWAS" and to build trust by "limiting the presence of external influences," which end up codified in the Declaration.

The discussions regarding treaty revision was the first instance where, collectively, ECOWAS member states committed to the transformation from an organization purely focused on economic integration and cooperation, to an organization focused on a more comprehensive form of political and sociocultural integration. Before discussing revising the treaty, ECOWAS member states who were also members of CEAO or the Mano River Union (MRU) would frequently obstruct progress toward ECOWAS goals such as trade liberalization. These countries filed for derogation from specific treaty provisions to preserve their arrangements in the other organizations. Representatives from Ghana, Nigeria, and Guinea argued that a new treaty should prioritize and elevate the activities of ECOWAS over other subregional memberships and the way to do so would be to broaden the scope of the organization.

The result was the creation of Article 4(a-k), which identifies a concerted effort to emphasize the good neighborness of ECOWAS member states, which is how they often referred to each other in both their official and informal dealings. Perhaps the most significant factor in this part of the ECOWAS treaty revision, along with the previous declaration of political principles, is that the organization, through these institutional changes, articulates a clear governance and government preference for its members. Thus, the organization would be responsible for determining and articulating the appropriate standards to be upheld by member states to be considered a good neighbor.

Another key treaty revision was codifying a decision-making mechanism within the organization, which was absent in the original 1975 treaty. Article 9(2) states that decisions in ECOWAS must be adopted by unanimity, consensus, or two-thirds majority of member states. Section 4 of Article 9 makes decisions binding on member states and institutions of ECOWAS.

Article 6 of the revised treaty reconfigures the institutions of ECOWAS and their functions. The institutions of the original treaty vested most of ECOWAS' operationalization in the Authority Heads of State. In the revised treaty, ECOWAS leaders resolved to create new institutions tasked with the day-to-day functioning of the community.

ECOWAS's first transformation provides important lessons in understanding institutional change, particularly regarding organizational problems of rule interpretation and enforcement. The Liberian Civil War is one example of how the interpretation and enforcement of the Mutual Assistance protocol and the contestation of its use opened up space for certain members to implement an existing institutional move in a new way. The treaty's revision was specific enough to retain certain aspects relating to the original mission of ECOWAS, particularly economic integration, but was ambiguous enough to allow for the organization to continue to adapt, expand, and reappropriate its goals as regional dynamics shift. An example of this institutional fluidity can be found in Articles 80–85 of the revised treaty, which further codify the rules of engagement between ECOWAS, non-state actors, other regional stakeholders, regional economic communities (RECs) and other international actors and task the coordination of these relationships to the Executive Secretariat. For example, Article 81 calls for the explicit involvement of regional stakeholders in the economic integration process, while never officially indicating how this would materialize.

From Response to Prevention: "The Mechanism"

Along with the revised treaty, there are two protocols associated with the first transformation of ECOWAS, which are crucial to understanding the organization's institutional development. The Protocol Relating to the Mechanism for Conflict Prevention, Management, Resolution, Peace-Keeping and Security commonly referred to as "The Mechanism" entered into force in 1999 and is instrumental in furthering ECOWAS' move toward a common position on democratic governance and peace and security. The Mechanism asserts that member states ought to commit to building stable democratic institutions within their member states. The Mechanism incorporates ECOMOG as the standing mediation entity in the region. It also commits member states to cooperation on the free movement of people, generating peace-keeping support for member states, safeguarding the cultural heritage of member states, and developing an ECOWAS standing army. The Mechanism calls for creating a mediation and Security Council, a subregional early warning unit, and the defense and security commission. The mechanism's significance to ECOWAS's first transformation is that it sought to create concrete preventative procedures and practices to facilitate changes within the member states. The protocol offers more specificity in ECOWAS' ability to intervene in member states, as stated in Article 25:

- In cases of aggression or conflict in any Member State or threat thereof;
- In case of conflict between two or several Member States;
- In case of internal conflict that threatens to trigger a humanitarian disaster, or that pose a serious threat to peace and security in the subregion;
- In event of serious and massive violation of human rights and the rule of law.
- In the event of an overthrow or attempted overthrow of a democratically elected government;
- Any other situation as may be decided by the Mediation and Security Council.

The Mechanism seeks to change institutional status quo by eliminating prior ambiguities of the rules around intervention by ECOWAS. More importantly, it also seeks to change institutional status quo by clearly positing the conditions under which member states will violate ECOWAS policy. Within this specificity are clear normative values that member states should seek to embrace, such as the rule of law, human rights, no unconstitutional changes in government, in addition to preexisting norms such as nonaggression within and between states.

The components of the mechanism demonstrate the deepening of the practice of intervention in West Africa. The practice of interference brings together the discursive and material worlds—interference as practiced in various ECOWAS interventions, through the interactions of ECOWAS Heads of States, and as codified in institutional protocols, the practice of interference becomes a routinized and regular action of the organization. The first transformation of ECOWAS builds on the founding conditions of unity through contestation and uses interference as a way to build a practical sense of what is appropriate among actors and enable the actors to develop understandings about the regional environment in a specific way. Specifically, the practice of interference is intentional in clarifying for regional actors that ECOWAS ought to develop the democratic principles to create stability in the region.

An example of how interference drives the regional pursuit of democratic governance is through the Supplemental Protocol of Democracy and Good Governance created and added on to the Mechanism in 2001. The protocol is notable for its strong stances on constitutional convergence among member states, election monitoring, preserving the rule of law, and the role of armed forces, police, and security forces in a democracy. The protocol also allows ECOWAS to sanction member states "if democracy is abruptly brought to an end" or if there is a humanitarian crisis in the member state.

ECOWAS' first transformation shows the process of evolution by an organization adapting to conflict-driven realities of West Africa, while trying to converge around ideals of democratic governance through the form of institutional change. However, this first transformation of ECOWAS highlights a tension between institutional convergence, normative convergence, and convergence in practice. Institutionally, ECOWAS was still very much "elite" dominated. Though with the development of the institutions created in the "Revised Treaty" and "The Mechanism" created new bureaucratic positions such as the ECOWAS Executive Secretary, much of the operational work was left for the Council of Ministers. They were appointed by their home governments, which posed human resource issues and issues of political will. According to Kebba Toure, an ECOWAS practitioner who was part of a contingent from Guinea on behalf of Prime Minister Lamine Sidime that worked on the implementation phase of the 2001 Supplemental Protocol, the council of ministers could not agree on how to disperse the revenue from the community levy, mainly because not every member state would contribute. Toure also cited how the Council of Ministers often took the position to advocate for their home governments, which led to stalemates in the implementation process.

Normatively, the first transformation indicated a concentrated desire to converge on democratic governance through the linkage of peace and security. One can trace the content of the institutional developments from the 1991 Declaration of Political Principles to the 2001 Supplemental Protocol and see how ECOWAS made a concerted effort to have issues of democracy and good governance incorporated into the institutional fabric of ECOWAS. What explains the commitment to democratic governance? One argument is that the pursuit of democracy and good governance is part of a larger strategy for heads of states to prop their regimes to look more legitimate to the international community and ensure authoritarian survival. By pursuing regional policies that amplify democracy and good governance, leaders can show support and loyalty for each other, which enables them to raise their profile, formal sovereignty, without ensuring that policies get implemented. However, the process and commitment to institutional reform and the debate by ECOWAS practitioners and ministers to create protocols that strengthen the material and discursive process of democracy indicate a desire to deepen democratic governance to improve the quality of life in the region. This view is bolstered by the fact that ECOWAS practitioners did not view the protocols and the treaty of ECOWAS as merely "words on paper"—ECOWAS practitioners believe that the protocols they sign and implement are meant to have deepening effects and foster cooperation. This is illustrated by one practitioner clearly:

> ECOWAS is set up to drive cooperation between member states, that is a given. However, it is not to just have agreement; we are committed to deepening cooperation. From the peace and security perspective, for us it is important to have adequate protocols and mechanisms, and I will tell you that ECOWAS is one of the institutions globally that has outstanding normative frameworks so there is basis there… [I]f you read them [protocols and mechanisms] they are rich. Now, people say "there is a lot of conflict in West Africa" but I always say there is a lot of "will" to address [it].
>
> We have seen ECOWAS facilitate the Liberia intervention, and that was the first anywhere in the world. In addition, we believe we have the responsibility to protect each time now and have been acting on that responsibility… For me, that is one way to facilitate cooperation, by having democratic institutions that speak to popular representation, even if part of electoral process that are flawed. This is one gift we have given to the region, the member states, and the people who need democracy.[4]

The institutional reforms in the first transformation are driven by an underlying logic that comes from a mutually constituted understanding of West African leaders of unity through contestation, which is motivated by the practice of interference present in the organization from its outset. The institutional changes also indicate a process of learning between actors in the region. Evidence of this learning can be found in the changing of the organizational structure of ECOWAS, and in the belief and commitment of those who work in ECOWAS to uphold the normative standards and frameworks created during the organizations' formative stages and that words without operationalization would render ECOWAS a fruitless project. ECOWAS practitioners believe it to be their normative obligation to develop member state buy-in and the human resources necessary to carry out the organizational mandate.

Second Transformation of ECOWAS: The Creation of the ECOWAS Commission

The period of the first transformation can be described as a period of big ideas. Much of the changes in the organization were reactions to events that occurred in the region, particularly the "big 3" interventions in Liberia, Sierra Leone, and Guinea-Bissau.[5] In an effort to better understand the obstacles of implementation, the Authority Heads of States began the discussions on changing the ECOWAS Secretariat, filled with lower level operational staff and an Executive Secretary without the ability to implement decisions. During summit meeting discussions, West African leaders justified the change in the organizational structure as a way to improve "the capacity of the organization to achieve and implement its strategic goals." The Authority Heads of State also viewed a more expansive administrative structure as a way to overcome one of the hurdles to facilitating regional cooperation, such as the existence of overlapping regional groups and different regional influences. While the intention of redesigning the ECOWAS Secretariat was to improve the organization's technical capacity, its effects transcend the technical components. ECOWAS held a series of meetings between 2003 and 2006 to decide on the structure of the Commission.

ECOWAS often drew from its experience in facilitating post–civil war peace and reconciliation in three of its member states weighed heavy in the process of creating the Commission. For example, the discussion over restructuring was the first time outside the dimension of civil war that the ECOWAS Council of Ministers started to consider what ECOWAS is doing for its citizens, by mainstreaming discussions about how ECOWAS could reach its citizens. The prevailing thought on a people-centric approach to ECOWAS was that changing the organizational structure would allow more citizens and regional stakeholders to be involved in the organization. Despite aspirations to reconsider ECOWAS as a purely state-driven regional project, the reconstruction discussions still wrestled with distributional concerns, primarily the perception of Nigeria as the most significant contributor to the community levy and the organization's military interventions. However, as restructuring advanced up the agenda of the Executive Secretary, the Council of Ministers, and the Authority Heads of States, Nigeria, to somewhat of a surprise, did not assume that a new organization would usurp its role in the organization.

Two current ECOWAS practitioners familiar with the restructuring recalled a proposal by Sierra Leone and Cote d'Ivorie for the commissioners to be representatives from each member state, and member states would be responsible for paying their commissioners. The current practitioners argued:

> This was a time for Nigeria to step up and assert its leadership as the hegemonic power in West Africa. It is in Nigeria's interest to have this structure. But what happens? Nigerian representatives present at the meeting did not say a word. Nigeria does not often assert themselves in ECOWAS. They did not want to be active and this is why we have the current structure [seven commissioners, paid for by ECOWAS].

The characterization of Nigeria as a passive actor during the restructuring of ECOWAS explains away notions of an insurmountable large state influence in the region, and the passiveness therein, and also provides an example of how the interactions of particular practices and practical sense can be mediating factors in institutional change. Suppose institutional change is an outcome of struggles that ultimately reflect inequalities of power. In that case, we can interpret Nigeria's "passiveness" as a corrective behavior to previous institutional contexts and behaviors that existed in the organization, particularly instances where certain member states would hold up integration initiatives to preserve their own interests.[6] Thus, the second transformation of ECOWAS was an attempt to build an institutional structure that did not privilege one country and its capabilities over another, for the sake of harmonization. The result is the passage of Regulation C/REG.706/07, Approving the Organizational Structure of the Commission of ECOWAS.

ECOWAS' second transformation is important in the institutional development of democracy and good governance for three reasons. First, the restructuring of the organization created an institutional apparatus and a significant amount of resources for peace and security issues and as mentioned above, the impetus to transform the organization was in response to the civil conflicts and challenges maintaining peace, security, democracy, and good governance in the region. One of the key institutional innovations in this area was the creation of the Political Affairs, Peace and Security commission (PAPS). PAPS consists of sub-divisions of Peacekeeping and Regional Security and Political Affairs and formerly Early Warning. According to ECOWAS strategic planning documents and budget reports from 2007 to 2013 as well as from 2013 to 2016, the Political Affairs Commission receives the largest percentage of ECOWAS funding. For example, in 2011–2015, 22% of the entire ECOWAS Commission budget ($28,797,393) was allocated toward "good governance" programs alone. These programs included the facilitation of the ECPF, capacity building for peace and security programs, establishment and support for national conflict prevention frameworks, and electoral observations. In addition, during 2011–2015, 26% of the entire Commission budget ($33,278,914) went toward implementing existing policies and protocols. The PAPS commission is both empowered and instrumental in all of ECOWAS' peace and security initiatives, and the organization allocates significant resources to stress the importance of Peace and Security to the region-building process. While ECOWAS was indeed innovative in creating mechanisms to respond to civil conflict in the region, the second transformation helps us understand how institutional change can lead to positive feedback mechanisms within an organization. It gives way to the slow-moving processes that lead to significant institutional change.

The second reason why this transformation is important is the creation of an institutional space that would allow commissioners and practitioners to be autonomous in the facilitation and harmonization of peace and security/democracy and good governance initiatives. The autonomy of ECOWAS practitioners is significant as they emerge as new actors with both symbolic and material effect associated with a transformed perception of the organization and offer an alternative actor to consider when measuring the progress and performance of democracy and good governance in the region.

Finally, the importance of the second transformation is that it offers the opportunity to examine institutional feedback through the earlier organizational shift from solely conflict resolution to conflict prevention. One of the first mandates of the PAPS commission was to build on earlier institutional protocols to develop a comprehensive framework for member states and regional peace and security stakeholders to follow, further entrenching and clarifying the appropriateness of interference in the region. What follows below is an examination of the ECPF, one of the first big institutional achievements of the ECOWAS Commission and a framework that first reflects the practitioner's articulation of ECOWAS' inclusion of regional stakeholders and civil society.

The ECOWAS Conflict Prevention Framework

The ECPF is a regulatory framework that combines the Mechanism's mandate and the newly established Peace and Security organs of the second transformation. The main component of the ECPF is to harmonize, facilitate, and advocate preventative action on peace and security by strengthening internal coordination within ECOWAS member states and relevant regional stakeholders, and better utilize the deployment of peace and security instruments. Mohamed Ibn Chambas, the first ECOWAS Commission President (and previously the ECOWAS Executive Secretary), made the ECPF part of his initial strategic agenda and stressed the inclusion of regional civil society in maintaining peace and security. Chambas' rationale was that the peace process in West Africa and therefore the emergence of democracy and good governance ought to be placed in the people's hand and the driver to move toward an "ECOWAS" of people. In practice, the ECPF would "resolve tensions between sovereignty and supra-nationality, and between regime security and human security," and these tensions would be resolved "in favor of supra-nationality and human security respectively." The purpose of the ECPF is to create more "effective and durable cooperative interventions to prevent violent conflicts within and between states" and to establish "conditions to eliminate the pervasive threats to people's and individual rights; the protection of human and democratic rights, and the promotion of human development to ensure freedom from fear and freedom from want." The ECPF focuses on two aspects of prevention: operational prevention, which consists of the methods and strategies used to halt conflicts from escalating to violence, such as early warning, mediation, preventative disarmament, and preventative deployment through the use of an ESF. The other is structural prevention through peacebuilding initiatives, political, institutional, and development reforms, and an enhanced capacity to design and advocate for a culture of peace in the region.

The ECPF encompasses more than just aggressive acts by dissident groups within or external to the state on the practice of interference. The ECPF also gives attention to the nonviolent conflict dimensions. During PAPS commission committee meetings on the ECPF, Dr. Cyriaque Agnekethom, the Director of Peacekeeping Department in the PAPS Commission, argued during the drafting of the ECPF in 2007:

> ECOWAS is at a comparative advantage in Africa. We have the resources here to affect the livelihood of West Africans, but we must make sure that this framework builds the capacity for the people to protect themselves against conflict and for the people to take ownership of their issues. It should be our role to help provide the structure and mechanisms that create an environment for peace and stability.

ECOWAS practitioners involved with the drafting of the ECPF viewed this strategy as a way to think beyond the organization's structural constraints and offered an opportunity for ECOWAS as an institution to imbue its community members with agency shape peace processes within the region. This is significant, given traditional peacebuilding, peacekeeping, and peace enforcement operations are initiated through the UN. The recognition and classification of the organization as having a "comparative advantage" indicates a cognizance and an embedded belief by practitioners that they can develop the capacity to continue to take ownership over the development of peace and security in the region. Moreover, stressing a comparative advantage demonstrates that the drafters of the ECPF were working off of the background conditions and experiences of ECOWAS forays into conflict prevention.

Aside from the lack of internal coordination to make previous protocols and decisions operational, there was no explicit link of previous conflict prevention/resolution practices to the agency or empowerment of ECOWAS citizens, evidenced by the emphasis on human security in the ECPF and the state-centric approaches in previous protocols. Further, the protocols passed during the first transformation did not include a prominent role for regional or local peace and security stakeholders, where the ECPF calls for a much more active involvement of these actors.

The ECPF was created not only by a mix of ECOWAS practitioners who were holdovers from the previous ECOWAS administrative configuration but also by practitioners who were working in places such as the UN, as international lawyers, or as staff in the previous secretariat, who had spent years in the region working on the ground and were able to bring their expertise to the drafting of the document and understood the previous context of unity through contestation. ECOWAS practitioners have a significant causal role in facilitating harmonization in peace and security. ECOWAS practitioners stressed in the drafting of the ECPF the need to create pathways for sustainable interactions toward the development of peace and security cooperation in the region. Numerous memos between the PAPS commission and the President of the Commission mentioned the "long-lasting effects" and "learning from the past" to build more "reliable structures of prevention." From this vantage point, ECOWAS practitioners sought to create a distinctly local meaning of peace and security and democracy and good governance. The ECPF created "orienting concepts" that mediated how member states and regional peace and security stakeholders should approach maintaining peace and security in the region.

Taken together, the institutional changes in ECOWAS from the Non-Aggression protocol, to the revised treaty, to the transformation to the Commission, and the creation of the ECPF, demonstrate a process of regional cooperation conditioned by both structural changes and eventually the agency of ECOWAS practitioners. The outcome of these institutional changes is a commitment to a more inclusive region-building approach that privileges the shared livelihood of people, the de-escalation and prevention of violent conflict in the region, and a more local, bottom-up approach to regional interactions that build trust among and between the citizens of West Africa. Through these institutional innovations and changes, ECOWAS practitioners emerge as the key actors to advocate, shape, and drive regional governance in peace and security, despite the assertion by the Authority Heads of State and Government vesting the responsibility for democratic governance and peace and security with member state governments.

The following sections will detail the practices ECOWAS practitioners use to facilitate and harmonize the region in democracies and good governance, including Regional Civil Society organizations in the governance process and the use of Memorandum of Understanding (MoUs) as tools to communicate and advocate for particular regional needs arrangements and relationships. These practices are examples of how practitioners display their agentic capacities use them as a tool to facilitate regional connections.

ECOWAS and Regional Civil Society

One of the outcomes of ECOWAS' second transformation was a move towards conflict prevention, which featured the inclusion of regional civil society organizations (RCSOs) in conflict prevention and democracy promotion efforts around the region, with the intention to incorporate more region-specific approaches and responses to conflicts in the region. One of the key partners of ECOWAS is the West African Network for Peacebuilding

(WANEP), a peace and security civil society organization established in 1998 with a mandate to provide active nonviolence training, peace education, and mobilizing special peacebuilding support across West Africa. ECOWAS and WANEP established an official relationship in 2004, through an MoU, which is renewed annually.

The initial MoU between ECOWAS and WANEP detailed the type of operational support that WANEP would provide ECOWAS, specifically in the area of early warning. The tenets of the MoU evolved to include WANEP's entrenchment within the ECOWAS Commission, establishing relationships with various departments including Political Affairs and Peace and Security, the Gender, Humanitarian and Social Affairs, and Environmental departments of ECOWAS. In 2014, the MoU deepened the relationship between ECOWAS and WANEP, creating a permanent position for a WANEP Representative to ECOWAS, with the goal of operationalizing and implementing a decentralized Early Warning and Response Network in West Africa, spearheaded by ECOWAS and WANEP, called "ECOWARN." The deepening of the relationship between ECOWAS and WANEP is attributed to a concentrated effort by the practitioners that made up the early warning directorate and their activism in framing both early warning and the role of civil society as crucial to conflict prevention and democracy promotion (Eze 2020).

One of the main individuals driving the relationship between ECOWAS and WANEP was Mrs. Onyinye Onwuka, former Head of Analysis in ECOWAS Early Warning Department. Mrs. Onyinye, a former senior research officer in the Ministry of Foreign Affairs in Nigeria, came to ECOWAS to work as a program officer in the Early Warning directorate, and was in charge of monitoring in Nigeria, Burkina Faso, and Niger and became Head of Analysis in 2014. Early Warning has three divisions: Analysis, Systems Analysis, and Communication and each division has a director. The Director of Analysis is responsible for generating early warning reports, forecasting, and management of early warning analysts on the ground. Practitioners in early warning assure that analysts are clustered into countries to assure that there is effective monitoring on the ground. Structurally, there are about 87 field monitors spread out across West Africa. ECOWAS provides each country with five field monitors, and WANEP provides the rest of the contingents in each country. Under Onyinye, the scope of early warning and monitoring expanded beyond country-based monitoring and moving toward thematic-based monitoring, while also deepening WANEP's role as an implementing partner.

Onyinye used her position to prioritize the importance of early warning as a core prevention strategy. Her position of deeply institutionalizing or embedding early warning in the organization beyond peace and security is informed by her background experience as a field monitor, particularly to deal with ECOWAS' capacity to respond to crises and adapt to emerging trends in the region. For example, when describing the threat of terrorism and violent extremism, she expresses that in order for ECOWAS to build a response to the threat of extremism adequately, it is necessary to go beyond naming the problem:

> [T]errorism is so important because it underlies many of the challenges we face. I am interested in understanding drivers. I am also interested in not just labeling why we have terrorism, but how are counter-narratives produced to de-construct very strict ideologies; how do you get people within communities vulnerable to being recruited, or brainwashed into joining terror groups. I want to make my contribution to the discussions and conversations around terrorism and want stakeholders to engage with me so they can understand from the ECOWAS perspective, our regional output.

ECOWAS practitioners of early warning, including Onwuka, often stress that a key hurdle to maximizing the effect of early warning in the region is implementation and capacity building. These are the key reasons why practitioners sought out WANEP as an "implementing partner." Typically, governments view civil society organizations as opposition members, reflected in the regulatory laws enacted by states to control their activities. The tensions between civil society organizations and governments are often a result of an organization's (in)ability to self-regulate and develop organizational standards that will avoid restrictive government regulation. Despite this dynamic, ECOWAS partners with WANEP for three reasons. First, WANEP is an African-created civil society organization. It was created to serve West Africans and build the capacity of West Africans to solve and prevent conflicts on their own terms. Second, through its work in early warning and relationship building within member states' national governments, WANEP has credibility as an organization throughout the region. For instance, the Executive Director of WANEP, Dr. Eze, states that WANEP makes a conscious decision to "accompany" the state, rather than inherently antagonizing national governments, which endears WANEP to the state as a partner, rather than an adversary. WANEP also has credibility because of its stability as an organization. WANEP's financial management, leadership and governance structure, and transparency as an institution give ECOWAS and its member states confidence in the ability and capacity of WANEP to be truly network based. To deepen the relationship between ECOWAS and WANEP, they created a new in-house liaison position in the 2014 MoU. This person would be based in Abuja at the ECOWAS Commission, responsible for facilitating the integration of civil society into early warning and contributing to the analysis and forecasting of Early Warning. In addition to this position, WANEP would also help spearhead the decentralization of early warning in ECOWAS member states.

Driving the efforts of WANEP and ECOWAS in building up the regional capacity and development of democracy and good governance as well as the maintenance of peace and security are the practitioners who create, shape, and facilitate the initiatives for connectivity. These practitioners are motivated primarily by their own lived experiences with conflict in their home countries and their desires to improve the dynamics in the region. For example, the current WANEP liaison officer to ECOWAS, Alimou Diallo, has nearly 20 years of experience in peacebuilding and joined WANEP as the country coordinator for Guinea in 2006. Diallo entered the work of peace and security via five years of work experience in a refugee camp providing humanitarian support for refugees from the Liberian and Sierra Leonean civil wars. When describing why he chose to enter the field of peacebuilding, he reflects:

> I saw firsthand what war can do to people. It rips them of their dignity and even within the refugee camp; refugees were so vulnerable that the camp management, security management, were not able to protect most of them. Since then, my work was to respond to people that have been affected by war and conflict. So I thought maybe the best way would be to change my career to focus on how to prevent conflict in the first place, instead of providing humanitarian services to victims of war and violence.

Diallo also mentioned that his work in Guinea as member of WANEP was to help strengthen its democratic governance, in the face of two long-term dictators. His role was to mobilize citizens through civic education and building the capacity for them to participate effectively in the election, to offset the risk of potential electoral violence. Diallo's role has since expanded since he arrived at ECOWAS as the WANEP liaison. Diallo is now the Chief of Party of the United States Agency for International Development (USAID) Reacting to Early Warning and Response Data (REWARD) initiative, where he also oversees election monitoring and facilitates social inclusion throughout the region.

One of the main practices that emerge out of ECOWAS and WANEP's partnership in early warning is the decentralization of the peacebuilding process. By decentralizing the process, ECOWAS and WANEP practitioners believe they can best incorporate local capacity building into the regional structure and plan for early warning, while vesting the responsibility and management of peace and security to civilians. ECOWAS practitioners in particular argue that decentralizing peacebuilding mitigates the gap between "alert" and "response" and limits the prospect of spillover that may impede any attempts at peacebuilding. One practitioner characterizes this gap between alert and response to be a symptom of the preservation of member state sovereignty. Their characterization mentions the issue of piracy in ECOWAS and tensions between Nigeria and Ghana despite calls for harmonization through the ECOWAS Integrated Maritime Strategy (EIMS), which initially limited the scope of how ECOWAS could respond to the issue.

In 2016, ECOWARN field officers in Ghana, Nigeria, and Togo surveyed the issue of piracy and conceived a menu of policy options, in an effort to build on the commitments to the EIMS. One of the policy options was to incorporate maritime stakeholders into the process of early warning by providing assistance with strengthening surveillance efforts in the Gulf of Guinea. These stakeholders included the UN office for Drugs and Crime (UNODC), the government of the United Kingdom, Centre for Maritime laws Africa (CEMLAWS), as well as the Economic Community of Central African States (ECCAS) and Gulf of Guinea Commission (GGC), which already had an established relationship through the Yaoundé Code of Conduct in 2013 and an MoU that established an Inter-Regional Architecture of maritime centers of excellence. ECOWARN benchmarked the capacity to provide comprehensive maritime security through a pilot early warning response mechanism program in Liberia, Mali, Guinea-Bissau, Burkina Faso, and Cote d'Ivorie. These national early warning centers would be to feed information about nascent and emerging conflicts within a country to the region and give national centers implementing power to create and quickly respond to imminent threats.

As a result of the benchmarking by ECOWARN and the inclusion of these stakeholders, the ECOWAS Commission established a comprehensive MoU for joint maritime operations in the Gulf of Guinea and enhanced the resources available to the Inter-Regional Architecture to mobilize national maritime structures in individual member states. The MoU highlights the need for collaboration and mobilization of resources related to collective security through joint and combined maritime operations against criminality, particularly the prevention of piracy, armed robbery, and attacks against ships and illicit activities.

ECOWAS practitioners as well as ECOWARN field officers view the practice of decentralization as an example of ECOWAS moving from an "ECOWAS of States" to "ECOWAS of People." They candidly state that this is their new orientation as a community of practice, to mitigate the gap of response by empowering local communities to take ownership of their conflicts. An ECOWARN field officer from Sierra Leone states that decentralization of peacebuilding can be a prototypical response mechanism that can improve coordination between member states while also improving the quality of early warning data available to the ECOWAS Commission. Numerous practitioners also cite how the use of MoUs to decentralize the peacebuilding process is a way to both bypass perceived infringement of sovereignty and better incorporate civil society into the response and implementing mechanisms at the national level.

The networking between ECOWAS and WANEP is an example of how particular practices, such as the use of MoUs and decentralization, can correct institutional constraints while also being informed and conditioned by past experiences in the organization. Whereas the capacity to respond to conflicts in the past was limited by uneven capacities and resources of ECOWAS member states, ECOWAS practitioners use MoUs as a tool to not only increase the material resources needed to manage and enhance peace and security but also deepen the relationships and interactions between those actors that ECOWAS chooses to engage with. The outcome of these practices is that it makes the early warning process visible and available to citizens on the ground. The networked relationship between ECOWAS and WANEP also has implications on processes of localization. For example, through decentralizing early warning, field officers offer local-driven responses to conflict in the national centers of early warning to incorporate indigenous conflict resolution mechanisms into their structures. A ECOWARN field officer points to the use of palava/peace huts as an example of an indigenous conflict prevention mechanism in Liberia.

Palava huts are small hamlets that are built in the middle of a village. The people in the village agree that whenever there is a problem, the Palava is the place where people should come and talk about it. These huts, which women in the community primarily organize, are important in promoting dialogue and mediation and represent a shared way of people taking ownership. Each peace hut has a register where one of the key tasks in conflict prevention by the national early warning centers is to ensure that these "peace huts" are plentiful in both urban and rural areas in member states. The palava huts are called "peace huts" to reorient the scope from conflict resolution to conflict prevention and serve as the "first response" to conflict. If the conflict is not criminal in nature, it is up to the registers of the huts to resolve the conflict there. If disputes are criminal, the registers are responsible for reporting the conflict to the appropriate local authorities. The peace huts are also places where women in particular have been able to generate income, engaging in activities such as tie-dyeing and soapmaking, with the idea that the peace huts have a more holistic function than just conflict prevention. They serve as hubs for community engagement, economic development, and capacity building, which can reduce the potential for small-scale conflict.

ECOWAS and WANEP have also worked to incorporate traditional leaders into conflict prevention at the country and regional level, as exemplified in creating the National Peace Council (NPC) in Ghana. The NPC includes traditional leaders and religious leaders in Ghana and started out as an informal structure used during elections to advocate for peace. WANEP, under a mandate from ECOWAS, worked with the Ghanaian government to formalize the NPC. WANEP played a significant role in drafting the concept note that went to the interior ministry and eventually turned into Act 818 to establish the NPC.

While the partnership between ECOWAS and WANEP has yielded positive impacts on the development of regional conflict prevention mechanisms, there are still various challenges in fully meeting the mandate based on the uneven role of civil society and indigenous and religious leaders. For instance, ECOWAS practitioners often compared the differences of religiosity between countries like Ghana and Cote d'Ivoire to judge the potential effectiveness of civil society in the respective member states. ECOWARN field officers frequently referenced the numerous consultative meetings held with WANEP with representatives in Cote d'Ivoire where the idea of an NPC, much in the same structure as Ghana, was proposed to traditional leaders. Traditional and religious leaders in Cote d'Ivoire argued that people are not religious, traditional leaders are not neutral, and civil society is polarized, conceiving any notion or idea of an NPC to be ineffective. They suggested that for an NPC to work in the country, political parties must be a part of it. ECOWARN practitioners viewed this to be problematic due to the fear that the NPC would devolve into another forum for political parties to push their agendas. ECOWARN's task has been to find a formula that can be replicated throughout the region and the start of convergence on a local level, that gives agency to civilians.

Through the establishment of national centers, early warning practitioners bring the region together by articulating practical and normative standards for engagement between civil society, member states, and their constitutive populations. The scope, depth, and effectiveness of the ECOWAS and WANEP relationship is a result of WANEP's established structure and credibility as a civil society organization in West Africa. By establishing concrete rules of membership, internal checks, and a path to leadership succession, WANEP is able to be a reliable partner to ECOWAS. WANEP is also aided by its position as a "meso"-level organization. It is not "macro" in a continental sense, local in a municipal sense, or national. As such, it has quality control over the organizations it partners with. For example, once a civil society organization becomes part of WANEP, it becomes beholden to the standards of the WANEP constitution and its structure. WANEP has a strict formula for entrance, and in countries where the civil society network is not strong or does not adhere to WANEP's constitution, they are expelled from the organization, and civil society organizations must start over again based on the policies of WANEP.

For organizations to become members of WANEP, they have to grade well on five components: institutional viability, legal environment, advocacy, financial means, and network capacity to deliver. Using an evidence-based approach, WANEP develops indicators used to monitor and engage policy makers and be transparent about the utility of their policy recommendations. Each of the national centers have evaluators who grade organizations from A to E. Organizations that are graded with the "A" and "B" categories have full autonomy to function because they have the structure and capacity to do so. Those with grades C–E have to consult with WANEP and receive approval from the regional secretariat in order to engage in early warning or other peacebuilding initiatives.

While the partnership with ECOWAS and WANEP provides a platform where civil society is coordinated and organized, cultural issues inhibit the effectiveness of the inclusion of civil society in regional peace and security governance. Many civil society organizations do not have the operational capacity to survive. In many West African countries, the relationship between civil society and the government is highly contentious. According to practitioners, the most effective relationships between ECOWARN and civil society are reflected in governance culture in a given country.

By focusing on a small number of programs or thematic areas, the ECOWARN partnership increases the capacity for policy implementation and gives each organization more credibility in the eyes of donors and in the communities they serve, while also empowering citizens in member states to take ownership over the responses to conflict—for example, during an intervention in the communal clash between the Mamprussi and Kusasi in Northern Ghana, an area with enduring tensions that required the Ghanaian government at one point to deploy the military to the region and establish a two-year curfew in Bawku in 2008. As part of the ECOWARN intervention, field officers removed the parties from the conflict zone and brought them to Kumasi, located in the Ashanti region of Ghana, and organized a series of dialogue sessions. Part of the negotiated peace agreement was the construction of a grievance wall within the town of Bawku, where, instead of fighting, they would write their grievances on the wall.

In fact, there was a festival that was coming up, and one party wanted to organize a festival, but the other party needed to agree to it, which they did not, initially. One guy wrote very insulting statements on the wall. When he called, he said,

> "you people said we should not fight, so I wrote on the wall to express myself ... instead of fighting this is what we are doing now." So we have to educate them and say that this is also not the way of dealing with it. This is to say that we have engaged in many communal conflicts and we are able to successfully resolve it. Up to now, they continue calling if there is any issue they will call WANEP. We set up a committee comprising all ethnic groups, including two parties that are in conflict. The two parties appointed a chief, who is a leader in that committee. So if there is anything they hear, the committee will meet first and decide before there is action. Initially, there was no mechanism for engagement so when something happens, people just go and retaliate. Whether it is a rumor or a real thing. Since there is this inter-ethnic committee, now they are managing their own lives. Since 2010 in Northern Ghana, the killing has diminished. There are tensions, but they are managing to live with it. And that's the idea of empowering communities, for them to see the dividends. They were campaigning for us to help lift the curfew and the riding of motorbikes. All of that was banned, We told them if they continue like this in the next year, we will intervene and talk to the government. When we are doing this, we do it with the involvement of parliamentarians from that region.

Since ECOWAS created a peace and security architecture, based on the experiences of the civil wars of the 1990s, there has been improvement on the capacity of ECOWAS to engage the region to deal with crisis. ECOWAS's increased capacity to respond on local levels has reduced the number of open conflicts in the region. The efforts to learn and improve upon the mistakes of the 1990s are driven by ECOWAS practitioners in peace and security, which can gather and disseminate information and resources to help quell conflicts. Why have ECOWAS practitioners taken the mantle to drive regional peace and security convergence on their own accord? The answer lies in the ability for ECOWAS practitioners to prioritize harmonization above institutional inertia and ineptness. Mrs. Onyinye mentions that her biggest challenge as program officer and monitor and Head of Analysis is getting the Authority Heads of State to acknowledge and act on the alerts by ECOWARN. For example, in 2009, ECOWARN's forecasts and analysis all suggested that the then President Tandja of Niger would look to reform the constitution six months before elections, and the Heads of State ignored the reports. In ignoring the reports, Niger suffered a constitutional crisis and coup. Onyinye describes the trouble of overcoming the heads of state through an example of a report done on former President of Burkina Faso, Blaise Compaoré:

> We were writing a report on the President of Burkina. Then the president of the Commission [Kadré Désiré Ouédraogo] was from Burkina. So we write this report and I was very brutal on him. But how can we send that kind of report to the President? So I sent it to my then director, and she looks at it and says "hmm very nice but we cannot take it up to him because that guy is not going to sit down there" and Blaise hears that he was sitting in and took that kind of decision. So what we now do is nuanced it and say he should continue to do his good work and consider leaving office. But what kind of good job was he doing? That's why we work with WANEP. The things we cannot say, they will say. We have the challenge of getting the type of response that we desire. But the other challenges we have, we're working to close them with the national early warning centers, such as getting information at the grassroots and working with other actors at the local level.

Along with the challenges above, ECOWAS and WANEP face the challenge of dealing with a fluid security environment. A common belief among ECOWAS practitioners is that violent extremism is the next biggest threat to regional stability. Even though ECOWAS can handle any tasks in the region, violent extremism can dilute any progress made on convergence. Even with these challenges, early warning still serves as an example of the convergence in the normative and substantive form across the region.

Turning motivation into practice: Regional Convergence and the ECOWAS Standby Force (ESF)

Part of the ECPF mandate is the realization of a standing army in ECOWAS, in the form of the ESF. ECOWAS has been trying to implement the ESF since the Mutual Assistance protocol in 1981 and more concretely through the Mechanism in 1999. The hurdle in creating the ESF has been the lack of availability of troops from member states, which was also because member states were not compensating their troops adequately to be a part of the ESF. Another hurdle was the lack of harmonization when it came to training. Individual member states were responsible for training their own contingents, and when ECOWAS troops were deployed into the civil conflicts of the 1990s, the differences and experiences in the combat were alarming, thus rendering many ECOWAS contingents useless in resolving conflicts. To amend these shortcomings, ECOWAS practitioners in drafting the ECPF and later through Mediation Committee meetings advocated hard for regional military education and exercises, with the inclusion of the military and policing units within member states. These training and military exercises would take place throughout the region to provide ESF troops an experience with different terrains and encourage ESF troops and police officers to learn more about their peers and conjure up a sense of regional purpose in their participation with ESF. However, regional convergence can also have some unintended consequences.

In December 2015, ECOWAS practitioners in PAPS reached out to the International Red Cross about collaborating and holding a weeklong workshop on integrating international humanitarian law into the ESF as a way to hold joint military exercises and harmonize training. The training had a mix of military captains and lieutenants in all 15 member states and police officers from seven member states. The workshop was highly reminiscent of a college classroom: ESF troops were parked in a hotel conference room for much of the education portion of the week. Each ESF troop member and civilian police officer had at least a tablet or laptop computer, which seemed to occupy the attention of many of the troops. The presenters from the International Red Cross, a human rights lawyer from Australia, and a program officer from Geneva also seemed professorial in one regard, yet parental in another. During the educational training, the presenters often seemed perturbed by the ESF troops and their lack of expedience and participation in the workshop, resulting in condescension. The presenters also used a lot of jargon, which seemed to confuse ESF troops as well.

The point of the workshop was to train ESF troops on the proper humanitarian classifications and rules of engagement with the onset of conflict throughout the region. The training provided, which was part of an ECOWAS/AU/UN collaborative curriculum on incorporating humanitarian law into the regional standby force, focused on definitional issues, such as defining who civilians were and what were the rules of targeting and distinction, and highlighting standard operation on detention. More broadly, the incorporation of humanitarian law into the practices of the ESF also exemplified institutional learning and an evolution from the shortcomings of the ECOMOG days. ESF troops were trained specifically on the value of humane treatment—prohibition of torture, rape, slave labor, and enforced disappearance, all of which occurred in ECOMOG-controlled areas in Liberia and Sierra Leone in the 1990s. However, while ESF troops participated in the training, they were also skeptical of its intended effects. An ESF troop from Gambia asked, if the training and military practices are meant to protect civilians, then "why were countries being sanction," while another police officer from Burkina Faso suggested that this training was "another product of the West." These claims and questions present an interesting paradox. On one hand, by the troops agreeing to participate in the training, they are agreeing that improvements are needed at the regional level to make an effective standby force. On the other, their relative apathy and lack of knowledge of seemingly rudimentary humanitarian and military knowledge also indicate that the method of convergence might not extend to the individual logics of the ESF. Thus, the process of convergence is represented well by the motivations of ECOWAS practitioners, yet the realization of their motivations is at best uneven. Yet the outcome of workshops such as the one mentioned here, while important, does not capture the essence of regional convergence. That ECOWAS practitioners thought to bring external actors to improve the practices of the ESF, coupled with the physical coming together of troops from member states to harmonize around their rules of engagement and participate in military exercises, indicates a shift in institutional logic and practice that was not present in the previous iterations of the organization.

Conclusion

Peace and Security is a bedrock of ECOWAS since its founding; however, the articulation and interpretation of its importance has been met with successes and failures. This chapter highlights how ECOWAS, through institutional evolution and the motivation of ECOWAS practitioners in peace and security, has worked to create a normative and practical environment in West Africa that induces political stability, frees the region of open conflict, and networks the region through the inclusion of civil society and local/indigenous mechanisms for peace. By exploring the evolution of ECOWAS through two transformations, I illuminated how the founding conditions of the organization gave way for an interpretation of noninterference that is particular to the context of West Africa and counters conventional perspectives of regionalism in West Africa that posit ECOWAS had a strict normative adherence to nonintervention and the interventions of ECOWAS were violations of regional and global norms of sovereignty. I argued that by looking at the process and periodization of ECOWAS, its protocols, and the substance therein, we can glean a perspective of regional convergence that emphasizes on how targeted motivations by ECOWAS practitioners actually help push the peace and security agenda beyond legal protocols and into preventative action and process-driven implementation. The examples of the partnerships between ECOWARN and WANEP, as well as the networking between the ESF and the International Red Cross, demonstrate how ECOWAS practitioners in peace and security have shaped the agenda through their respective issue linkages to put an ECOWAS of people into practice, while strengthening the capacity and discursive value of its normative frameworks.

The role of ECOWAS practitioners in peace and security is vital to understanding how modes of behavior become embedded and normalized into ECOWAS and how these modes of behavior are a qualitatively different realization of regionalism in Africa than normally depicted. While conventional approaches to regionalism in Africa often stress the illiberal character and weakness of states, coupled with rampant political instability, driven by self-interested elites (Herbst 2007), the perspective provided here stresses the importance of analyzing regionalism in West Africa through the scope and complexities of all interactions, rather than a purely statist analysis. Admittedly, one may argue that by looking solely at how ECOWAS practitioners craft their own responses to region-building, the analysis misses the significant impacts of meso-level governance and the interactions with other informal sources of political and social life. However, I would argue that ECOWAS practitioners' role and their process of reaching local communities to facilitate convergence helped them become engaged with meso-level actors. The national early warning centers, for example, would not only be a way by which ECOWAS practitioners generate information, but their use as sites for conflict prevention for all members of a community can also shed light onto informal actors that might not have been readily known if early warning was not decentralized.

The lesson of peace and security in ECOWAS can also serve as an example of process-driven regional convergence in other subregions in Africa. Scholars of the East African Community (EAC) and the Southern African Development Community (SADC) for example, might understand how the evolution and transformation of the respective organizations remade themselves to improve upon the technical capacity of peace and security. Process-driven regional convergence in peace and security also eschews analyses that posit regional differences between heads of states to be the primary hurdles to regional convergence; rather, it focuses the attention on how the organization works to overcome such hurdles while simultaneously connecting and stabilizing the region through engagement with citizens and communities. With events such as Brexit potentially signaling a diffusion of disenfranchisement within societies, focusing on how modes of democratic governance as a normative and substantive preference are embedded in the region can provide a blueprint for other regions in Africa to develop policies or enable their practitioners to bridge the link between ordinary citizens and regional responses to governance.

Notes

1 The term "recycled elites" originates from Chabal and Daloz and their discussion on turnover of political leadership in Africa being extremely limited.
2 ECOWAS Protocol on Non-Aggression.
3 The Nigerian Observer Archive August 1990.

4 Interview, ECOWAS Practitioner, Political Affairs and Peace and Security, October 2019.
5 Adekeye Adebajo (2002). *Building Peace in West Africa: Liberia, Sierra Leone, and Guinea-Bissau*. Boulder, CO: Lynne Rienner Publishers.
6 Avelino, Flor, and Jan Rotmans (2009). "Power in Transition: An Interdisciplinary Framework to Study Power in Relation to Structural Change." *European Journal of Social Theory* 12(4): 543–569.

Bibliography

Adebajo, Adekeye. 2002. Building Peace in West Africa: Liberia, Sierra Leone, and Guinea-Bissau. Boulder, CO.: Lynne Rienner Publishers.

Adler-Nissen, Rebecca, and Alena Drieschova. 2019. "Track-Change Diplomacy: Technology, Affordances, and the Practice of International Negotiations." International Studies Quarterly 63(3): 531–545.

Ateku, Abdul-Jalilu. 2020. "Regional Intervention in the Promotion of Democracy in West Africa: An Analysis of the Political Crisis in the Gambia and ECOWAS' Coercive Diplomacy." Conflict, Security & Development 20(6): 677–696, DOI: 10.1080/14678802.2020.1854954

Adebajo, Adekeye. 2002. Building Peace in West Africa: Liberia, Sierra Leone, and Guinea-Bissau. Boulder, CO: Lynne Rienner Publishers.

Avelino, Flor, and Jan Rotmans. 2009. "Power in Transition: An Interdisciplinary Framework to Study Power in Relation to Structural Change." European Journal of Social Theory 12(4): 543–569.

Bareebe, Gerald. 2018. "The Pan-African Solidarity Norm". In African Actors in International Security: Shaping Contemporary Norms, eds. Katharina P. Coleman and Thomas K. Tieku. Boulder, CO: Lynne Rienner, 73–93.

ECOWAS Practitioner. 2019, October. Political Affairs and Peace and Security. Interview.

Eze, Chukwuemeka B. 2020. "Civil Society Organisations and the ECOWAS Peace and Security Agenda: A Case Study of the West Africa Network for Peacebuilding (WANEP)." In Regional Economic Communities and Peacebuilding in Africa: Lessons from ECOWAS and IGAD, eds. Victor Adetula, Redie Bereketeab, and Cyril Obi. London: Routledge, 68–81.

Hartmann, Christof. 2017. "ECOWAS and the Restoration of Democracy in The Gambia." Africa-Spectrum 52(1): 85–99.

Jalloh, Mohamed. 2014 "Regional Economic Integration and Incomes Convergence: A Case Study of the Economic Community of West African States." Journal of Economics and Sustainable Development 5(28): 81–93.

Kaboré, Dayog Néwndé. 2018. "ECOWAS's Leadership in the 2016th Gambian Post-Electoral Crisis – Challenging the UNSC's Primacy in Providing for Peace?" Archiv Des Völkerrechts 56(1): 71–95.

Klein, Robert. 1974. Sovereign Equality among States: The History of an Idea. University of Toronto Press.

Soyibo, Adedoyin. 1997. "Financial Liberalisation and Bank Restructuring in Sub-Saharan Africa: Some Lessons for Sequencing and Policy Design." Journal of African Economies 6(1): 100–150.

4 Regional Convergence in Public Health

On August 8, 2014, the World Health Organization (WHO) declared the Ebola outbreak in West Africa a "public health emergency of international concern," a rare designation by WHO. The Ebola outbreak, which began in December 2013 in Guinea, West Africa, was originally difficult to identify by health officials, and it rapidly spread throughout Guinea and into neighboring countries such as Liberia and Sierra Leone, eventually reaching Nigeria, Senegal, and Mali. The responses to the Ebola crisis from the international community and affected governments were varied. WHO was slow to coordinate intervention efforts among its designated response mechanisms (notably, WHO's Regional Office for Africa (AFRO)) and other international Non-governmental Organization (NGOs) such as Medicines Sans Frontiers/Doctors Without Borders (MSF). The governments of the affected West African countries were also confronted with the realization that their national health infrastructures were ill-equipped to respond to the Ebola outbreak and its rapid rate of contagion. The United States Government, the United Nations (UN), and thousands of public health NGOs deployed into West Africa to contain Ebola and "protect" the citizens of the afflicted West African nations.

Absent from many stories and coverage from the Ebola outbreak is the role and responses of ECOWAS and the context for understanding how and why West African countries were ill-equipped to deal with the scale of the Ebola outbreak, beyond the functions of institutional failures, cultural practices, or individual behaviors (Benton and Dionne 2015). The presence of ECOWAS is left out of the narratives on how the international community and West Africans themselves battled to overcome Ebola. The characterization of West Africa's health system is constrained by governance issues, low supplies of medical products, and poor cross-border cooperation to contain epidemics. As such, the Ebola crisis illustrates why the region and regional organizations are vital to improving the livelihood of West African countries.

What explains the disconnect between global and local responses to public health crises? Broadly, there is little formal coordination between WHO and ECOWAS. While WHO has the Africa Regional Office (WHO AFRO), which facilitates the inclusion of local (African-based) experts into WHO processes,

DOI: 10.4324/9780429436734-4

WHO integration into regional health governance schemes has been limited. Further, WHO advocates for country-driven health service provision, potentially creating inconsistencies in capacity and ability to deliver health services within Africa. Examining the regional level of interaction in health governance provides a lens that helps reconcile the disconnect between the global and regional scales of governance. A centering of regional health governance underscores how regional organizations and their component parts mediate interactions between global actors, regional actors, and non-state actors (Dodgson and Lee 2002). Additionally, it is important to understand how regional health governance is networked throughout the West Africa to identify the drivers or the delimiters of regional health convergence. In locating and highlighting the importance of the region in health, particular and significant cultural and social characteristics of the drivers of convergence become more salient and prevalent when identifying strategies and tactics of response.

This chapter examines regional health governance convergence, defined as the process in which regional political and social practices are harmonized and become more constant over time. Regional health convergence occurs by forming and creating social and political networks within and between ECOWAS and regional stakeholders in West Africa. This chapter makes the argument that the networks formed through the process of regional health convergence build acceptable, durable, and dependable modes of behavior in public health in West Africa. Regional health governance in West Africa is a process-driven project, facilitated by autonomous ECOWAS practitioners, actors within the ECOWAS bureaucracy who work on the day-to-day operations of ECOWAS in a specialized capacity. Regional health governance convergence occurs through the cooperation and networking of health-related civil society organizations and an ECOWAS-based health community of practice, tasked with harmonizing universal health practices across the region. Through the processes of regional health convergence, practitioners are empowered through the institutional changes within ECOWAS to shape institutional coordination of regional health actors in West Africa.

This chapter addresses two broader issues of regional health governance. First, the chapter is concerned with how ECOWAS facilitates the convergence of regional health practices in West Africa and with identifying how the actors that drive regional convergence use particular practices to inform processes of institutional change. Second, by examining networked regional governance in West Africa, the chapter moves away from conceptions of regional institutional change or stasis as determinant of regime boosting or a series of shadow activities by self-interested heads of state. Instead, the processes of regional health convergence demonstrate how autonomous actors such as health practitioners, when given the institutional space, work to determine what relationships and practices become embedded and should be made necessary within West Africa. The scope of this chapter is to understand the ways in which ECOWAS practitioners have worked on networking the region in public health, while highlighting how the framing and social context of public health become part of the strategy and normalized practices and policies of ECOWAS.

Regional convergence in public health provides a glimpse into the modes and methods of building health infrastructure in West Africa, defined here as the active construction of building frameworks for sustainable health services to deal with not only emergencies like Ebola but also diseases like NCDs and HIV/AIDS.[1] Public health issues across the continent in Africa are growing in scale. For instance, according to the World Bank, non-communicable diseases are the second leading cause of death in Africa. Africa also has the highest regionally concentrated diabetes mortality rate in the world, while the COVID-19 pandemic of 2020 has put an increasing amount of stress on the capacity of African health systems. A focus on a regional scale of health governance offers an opportunity to assess regional responses and assess the steps taken by actors on a regional scale, and to address proactive versus reactive planning.

Exploring the processes and activism of ECOWAS health practitioners also provides insights into the agentic capacities of actors outside of a state-centric framework. Take, for instance, African state responses to HIV/AIDS. In global health diplomacy, African states are both subject to dependency and demonstrate agency (Patterson 2018, 44). African states lack agency in that they are compelled to follow mandates from groups such as WHO and United Nations Programme on HIV/AIDS (UNAIDS) in order to delimit HIV prevalence. However, African states have agency within these contexts to shape and alter the narrative around response; they are able to advocate for resources using their intimate knowledge of what is necessary on the ground and give states the ability to create and build country-specific policies, with their own protocols to mitigate health issues.

The chapter proceeds in four parts. First, I situate the relevance of public health and regionalism, addressing the extent to which health is integrated into regionalization schemes, with a focus on the lack of bottom-up approaches to public health regionalism. Second, I briefly provide a context for public health in West Africa, highlighting the pervasiveness of communicable diseases, providing a basis for understanding the perceptions of public health in ECOWAS. Third, I explain the process of regional convergence in ECOWAS, by tracing the Bamako Initiative in 1987, where WHO and the United Nations Children's Fund (UNICEF), in conjunction with African Ministers of Health agreed to develop comprehensive strategies to increase access to primary health care by creating minimum health care packages that met community health needs. From this vantage point, I will highlight how the convergence of health practices develop as a localized mechanism to facilitate community health service provision. I provide evidence that emphasizes how the perceptions of public health in ECOWAS are manifested through the substance of Memorandum of Understanding (MoU), the creation of ECOWAS-driven public health networks, and the integration of civil society organizations into ECOWAS' health infrastructure. Finally, I offer implications regarding the need for increased institutional coordination in regional public health, particularly incorporating regional shared knowledge and existing convergence practices into the realm of public health into other pertinent areas of ECOWAS.

Regionalism and Public Health

As the 2014 Ebola outbreak in West Africa demonstrated, health crises could ravish the livelihood of people rapidly. The region becomes more important when considering the increased interconnectedness of people via the free movement of people and the proliferation of transborder issues that span and can transform the nature of governance. In the context of West Africa, the history of civil and ethnic conflict, post-electoral violence, play an important role in the ability for states and other actors to respond, prevent, and deliver health services to civilians. In acknowledging the inherent complexities of global health governance, articulating the role of the region is necessary for a number of reasons. First, using the region as the focal point brings to bear the scope and scale of health crises that span beyond the state. State-centric approaches to health governance focus on responses and prevention measures contained within state borders. Because of the scale and potential of spill over, responses to pandemics necessitate coordination beyond state borders. Second, the region, especially in the context of West Africa, presents a form of "locality"—meaning that the actors best suited to understanding the logistical and cultural contexts during pandemics and/or emergency crises come from West African states, rather than external health NGOs and Civil Society Organizations (CSOs). Finally, the region becomes important for geographical reasons. West Africa's most populous cities are on the coast and are subject to transience. As ECOWAS continues to move the region toward free movement of goods and people, the chances of exposure to diseases and sickness increase. A regional approach to health becomes more important in that it creates standardized methods of treatment and medical practices for citizens throughout the region. The ideal of a regional health infrastructure is that as West Africans have the ability to travel from Ghana to Cabo Verde, they should be able to receive the same type of health care/treatment that they would receive from their country of origin.

According to Dodger et al. (2002, 7), health governance refers to the rules, actions, and means by which society organizes itself in the promotion and protection of health in its population. As such, public health has become a priority for regional organizations, particularly in the Global South. Organizations such as ECOWAS and SADC in Southern Africa have realized that diseases like diabetes and HIV/AIDS are inextricably linked to political and economic development. Understanding the strength viability of the West African regional health infrastructure is a component piece to the building of regional health governance in West Africa. One can measure the durability of West Africa's regional health infrastructure in terms of its capacity-building mechanisms, the scope of its knowledge base, and its response mechanisms. While the structural durability of health infrastructure is important, the agentic factors are significant as well. In identifying the process by which health practitioners can build regional health infrastructure, we understand the social context in which practitioners develop their responses to crises and how they identify what to prioritize in the absence of crises. Also, by understanding the value ECOWAS practitioners place on building regional health infrastructure, evidenced through network formation and deep institutionalization of health practices, we can center the activism of regional health actors and networks to situate ECOWAS as an active contributor to health governance in West Africa, rather than a passive actor susceptible to the whims of misaligned priorities of governments and international organizations.

Beyond the issues of capacity building, efficacy of health systems, and knowledge formation, regionalism and health are linked for other reasons. In conflict-prone societies, health facilities are protected under international humanitarian law (Benton and Atshan 2016). West Africa's civil war history, particularly in Liberia and Sierra Leone, has left health facilities vulnerable to attack and populations ravished with poor health systems. As improvements in the area of peace and security increase, the relevance of public health increases. The remnants of war and famine provide increased opportunities for exposure to airborne diseases in the short/immediate term, and malnutrition can lead to short- and long-term health deficiencies. The Ebola Virus crisis of 2014–2015 saw most of its cases linked to intimate interpersonal contact—primarily handling dead bodies and preparing bodies for burial (Benton 2014). Similarly, the United States and Doctors Without Borders called for military troops on the ground to intervene in the Ebola crisis (Benton 2014; Rock and Focus 2014). The process of region-building advances a greater understanding of how and why actors within the region can develop strategies to link the priorities on the ground to the priorities of actors external to the region to achieve mutual benefits. The dynamics between the regionalization of health infrastructure and other facets of region-building such as peace and security also highlights how global south regionalisms are engaging in their own agentic political and social epistemic and power processes that respond to the imposition of external actors.[2]

The merits of regionalizing health governance provide greater "ease and pace" in agreeing on common social policy and provide a greater chance for regionally defined social standards (Riggirozzi and Yeates 2015). The drivers of regional health governance identify the "ease" and determine the "pace" of regional health infrastructure building. Regionalization of global health focuses on the capacity of regional organizations to work as blocs to adhere to policies of highly centralized global health international multilateral institutions (Riggirozzi and Yeates 2015, 220–221). Regional health infrastructure building in ECOWAS builds on this perspective and focuses on the agentic capacity of regional health practitioners and their ability to create networks with civil society organizations as well as multilateral institutions to garner support for its own agenda on facilitating regional health infrastructure building. Put differently, ECOWAS practitioners, through their autonomous position, contrive regional health policy and strategies, and use their self-cultivated networks to create regional health standards, response and prevention capacity, and knowledge formation. The creation of their own networks and knowledge formation are important to discern the intersubjective meanings of socialization around health. The rest of the chapter will provide the context as to how ECOWAS helped build a networked response to top-down prescriptions of health governance.

The Bamako Initiative: Founding Conditions of Public Health Convergence

The Bamako Initiative (BI) was a joint effort between the WHO and the UNICEF in 1987 aimed at improving the standards of health practices and access to health across Africa.

At its core, the Bamako Initiative was a move to create a structure for poverty-stricken populations in the global south that allowed communities to take ownership of their own health care systems. As intended by WHO and UNICEF, the Bamako Initiative classified health care as a means to reduce regional poverty. The idea of the Bamako Initiative was to put health back into the hands of the community while also embracing local traditions and approaches to health care. The intention of the Bamako Initiative suggested that when money from donor countries ran low or ran out, community-managed health care would create financial autonomy, relieving dependency on foreign sources of health care finance. West African governments at this time believed in the Bamako Initiative, as it allowed leaders to avoid questions of responsibility, particularly the role of the state. As one former deputy in the Nigerian Ministry of Health (now working in the West African Health Organization (WAHO)) intimated:

> Of course [Nigeria] wanted Bamako. This was the era of [former military President of Nigeria, Ibrahim Babaginda] where deregulation was the norm. Everything that could be left to localities, were. We were doing [structural adjustment programs] with the IMF and World Bank and while our economy grew, no money was spent on public sector programs, particularly education and health.[3]

The Bamako Initiative was also designed to benefit the enduring role of international organizations and their management of health care. There was the desire from WHO and UNICEF to generalize the micro experiences of community health. For example, when drafting the Bamako Initiative, WHO officials argued that community-based distribution of drugs, particularly by management committees, could have a positive effect on the control and distribution of illicit drugs on the local level (Ridde 2011).

It was the role of the Bamako Initiative to, in essence, become a "bottom-up" program—a program that left financing and health governance to the community level within states. However, in practice and operation, this did not occur. One of the more significant hurdles to implementation was the assurance that the poorest of poor would have access to health care by abolishing user fees. Countries were tasked to empower communities to involve consumers in the financing and managing of health services; however, countries in West Africa did not do the work to empower community-based health providers with a sense of ownership over the provision of health. More specifically, women were routinely left out of implementation of the Bamako Initiative, which was particularly alarming, given the proximity of women to health service at the household and community level. The Bamako Initiative also tasked communities to improve equitable access to essential drugs, especially by creating community financing structures that made health care free for those who truly could not afford it while those within the rest of society would participate in cost-sharing programs (WHO/UNICEF 1987). Local capacity to produce and purchase high-quality drugs at reasonable prices was weak, and health practitioners charged with implementing the Bamako Initiative did not do much to generate trust over the provision of generic drugs (WHO 1991). Operationally, communities were to implement the Bamako Initiative by national governments and/or external aid donors were to provide drugs to local health institutions and communities were to sell drugs at a small profit margin. The proceeds from drug sales were meant to replenish drug stocks, and the profits were to be used to improve the services of the health institution (Chukwuani et al. 2006).

The Bamako Initiative had varied success within Africa; however, as many health officials and researchers would note, many West African countries would experience problems with implementation. Some believe that the implementation problems came from a lack of policy coordination (Chukwuani et al. 2006; Nyonator et al. 2005). Target areas for the Bamako Initiative were mostly rural areas and relied primarily on volunteer services by village health workers, rather than certified health care professionals. Health ministries in the early implementing stages of the Bamako Initiative struggled to coordinate policies on how and which health workers would be available to distribute basic health services, leading to confusion by clients as to who and when health services would be provided to them (Nyonator et al. 2005). A health official from Burkina Faso explained the dynamics of community-based health "unreliable" and qualms:

> Unless you were in Ouaga (dougou) or even Bobo (Diassalou), it could take up to five days to know when and where clinics would be open. If you lived on the Togo-Benin Republic border, you would see lots of trafficking of prescription drugs because of this uncertainty.[4]

This sentiment from the health worker is substantiated by research on the effect of community-based health insurance and the utilization of health care services in Burkina Faso, which finds low numbers of Burkinabe citizens who report and seek health care, regardless of whether or not they have insurance. Further, the research found that socioeconomic means such as per capita expenditure and head of household education also correlated with a household's decision to enroll and participate in community-based insurance (Gnawali et al. 2009). In highlighting this dynamic in Burkina Faso, it shows that the Bamako Initiative, though meant to be a "bottom-up" policy in theory, presents some of the inconsistencies and unintended consequences of policies made to aid the Global South. It is also clear that it is the perception of health officials in West Africa that Bamako was a "product of the West" and there is an inherent of disdain and distrust of policies such as the Bamako Initiative primarily because it came from WHO. As such, the Bamako Initiative did suffer from issues of policy implementation, a lack of understanding of how rural communities would develop the capacity and the national support for community-based health initiatives, but also a lack of an inherent understanding as to how West African communities would respond and accept community-based health services as a practice.[5]

The analysis of the ineffectiveness of the Bamako Initiatives in many ways generalizes its effects across West Africa. The Bamako Initiative was successfully implemented in some places, notably in Ghana and its establishment of the Community Health Planning and Services Initiative (CHPS; Nyonator et al. 2005). However, in highlighting implementation problems with the Bamako Initiative, it is important to emphasize the void and the shortcomings of a global health practice that a particular region seemed to reject in substance and principle. Zooming out from the intricacies of implementing the Bamako Initiative in West Africa, we can see broader trends of a disconnect in disposition from WHO toward the West African region. Talking points from a meeting between African Heads of States and the WHO Director General, Dr. Hiroshi Nakajima reflected a WHO that did not focus on how to reach communities and provide guidance on how to implement its policies, but rather a WHO that was focused on linking economic and political development to health. Further, WHO would promise to recruit or send technical advisers to administer support to West African states, but would later curtail their commitment based on "extremely difficult political and economic conditions" (WHO 1988). For example, in order to facilitate the essential drug programme of the Bamako Initiative, WHO would provide essential personnel to help oversee and develop health systems and encouraged member states do develop state capacity around this support. Countries such as Guinea-Bissau followed suit, creating a Technical Committee within its Ministry of Health to include WHO, UNICEF, and NGOs' representatives. However, WHO never provided the resources it promised, often tethering their decisions to a need for further evaluation. West African nations did not hesitate to call out WHO representatives on this behavior. For instance, during the Thirty-Fifth Session of the WHO African Regional Committee, the Minister of Public Health, Social, and Women Affairs of Togo called out WHO for its political responsibility to the African region and chastised its use of resources in an "ad-hoc, short-term manner." The limited engagement and overpromising from WHO seemed to be all too familiar for West African health practitioners. West African health practitioners often cited how WHO was given an unprecedented opportunity to show the full range of its capabilities in improving the health systems in Africa, yet the organization never seizes the opportunity. As noted again by the Togolese Minister of Public Health, who accused WHO of seeing itself as a "donor and not a partner" and in doing so, WHO misuses its resources.

The lack of WHO buy-in on the Bamako Initiative provided an opportunity to advocate for themselves and hold WHO accountable by specifically placing the lack of implementation of the Bamako Initiative on WHO, while also highlighting how African nations can and should take ownership and management over decentralization of health systems. The frequent framing of WHO as "your" organization—as if to say, not an organization that serves or benefits African nations, signified a weariness of African health professions who did not want to depend on WHO but rather work in concert with WHO. More specifically, West African Health officials and the heads of state in ECOWAS decided to create their own regional health organization just one month after the signing of the Bamako Initiative as a means to collective will to embedded issues of public health, particularly the dissemination of knowledge about public health into regional integration strategies. The creation of the WAHO directly after the adoption of the Bamako Initiative is indicative of a desire by West African countries to assert their role of the region by articulating preferences of national governments when it comes to health and questions how the drivers of regional convergence articulate practices of region-building in health in West Africa.

Regional Convergence of Public Health in West Africa

Collaboration on public health in West Africa extends back to the colonial period, where Directors of Medical Services in Nigeria, the Gold Coast, and Sierra Leone would infrequently meet to exchange views on common health problems and the control of infectious diseases. These infrequent meetings transformed into the development of a West African Medical Research Council, which was part of a larger regional research coordination platform that included the West African Cocoa Research Institute, a currency board, and a court of appeals. While many of these research coordination efforts were dismantled in the postindependence period, countries such as Nigeria, Ghana, Gambia, Sierra Leone, and Liberia continued their collaboration through the Commonwealth Secretariat and its "Commonwealth Initiative," in 1965, which encouraged its members to build centres of excellence for medical teaching and research-building on what already existed. From here, Nigeria, Ghana, The Gambia, and Sierra Leone coordinated to create what became known as the West African Post-Graduate Medical College.

In 1972, the Commonwealth West African Regional Health Secretariat was established by Nigeria, Ghana, Sierra Leone and The Gambia, later transforming into the West African Health Community in 1978. The stated objectives of WAHC were to promote activities that strengthened health infrastructure and education through facilitated cooperation between member states and international health agencies, while establishing and building specialized technical capacity. The organizational structure consisted of an Executive Director, based in Lagos, an Assembly of Health Ministers, who serve as the governing council, an executive board, responsible for policy and management, and the secretariat, responsible for administration and coordination. WAHC also consisted of several specialized agencies, such as the West African College of Physicians, West African College of Surgeons, which was inclusive of francophone practitioners, and West African Pharmaceutical Federation, and embedded the West African Health Examinations Board into the organization as an ad hoc committee.

WAHC served as a specialized technical unit autonomous from the Commonwealth and was often portrayed as a partner agency of ECOWAS. The Executive Director served as the official liaison with UN agencies such as WHO, United Nations Development Programme (UNDP), Food and Agriculture Organization (FAO), and UNICEF, among others, as well as national agencies such as United States Agency for International Development (USAID), Canadian International Development Agency (CIDA), and African agencies such as ECOWAS, and the OAU. WAHC would later merge with the *Organisation de coordination pour la lute contre le grandes endeme*s (OCCGE), a dedicated Francophone West African health community based in Bobo-Dioulasso, Burkina Faso, and aimed at tackling tropical and infectious diseases.

On June 9, 1987, the Authority Heads of States in ECOWAS signed Protocol A/P2/7/87 establishing the WAHO, which was designated as a specialized institution of ECOWAS. WAHO's objective is to ensure

> the attainment of the highest possible standard and protection of health of the peoples in the sub-region through the harmonization of the policies of the Member States, pooling of resources, and cooperation with one another and with others for a collective and strategic combat against the health problems of the sub-region.
>
> (WAHO 1987, Article III)

WAHO was a product that was three years in the making, as noted in the ECOWAS Community Decision C/DEC.1/1184 that called for the integration of WAHC and OCCGE into one specialized institution in ECOWAS. WAHO was tasked, among many other things, to serve as a forum for collecting and disseminating technical and epidemiological research (Article III (c)), to train health care professionals, especially postgraduates and undergraduate (Article III (b)), to eradicate the use of and dependence on drugs and drug abuse (Article III (f)), and to promote and harmonize the establishment and production of vaccines, the manufacture of drugs, and the quality control of laboratories in West Africa (Article III (e)).

The establishment of WAHO came when ECOWAS as an organization was receiving criticism for its slow progress on economic integration. At the same time, civil conflict in Sierra Leone and Liberia were brewing, and Nigeria had recently experienced a military coup. ECOWAS had also been questioned by Francophone member states as to its relevance, as Francophone West African states were very much tied to its own monetary union, UEMOA. With regional leaders desiring to make ECOWAS a more expansive entity, health as part of the ECOWAS agenda can be traced to a series of meetings by West African Health ministers referenced in ordinary meetings of the Authority Heads of State in 1983. Public health was deemed a "vital component to poverty reduction and stable economic growth" in West Africa. The decision to engage in public health and create a specialized health agency in West Africa also came at the same time ECOWAS aimed to increase its cultural relevance in the region. Most of the commentary at the ordinary meetings of ECOWAS in 1985 and 1986 was focused on enhancing ECOWAS' desire to define itself not only as an economic organization but also as an organization that had a common culture. Hence, alongside the creation of the WAHO came Protocol A/P1/7/87 establishing the Cultural Framework Agreement in ECOWAS. The principles of this agreement were to promote the cultural identity of respective people and for ECOWAS to understand cultural identity as a "dynamic process of continuity and creativity, which is different in each population (ECOWAS 1987). Articles 5 and 6 of the Cultural Framework Protocol apply the principles of the cultural framework to areas of "sociocultural development" such as education, child development, literacy, and health. In particular, Article 6(7) calls for the training of rural professionals and to link cultural development with the improvement and integration of rural communities.

The linkage between the Protocols establishing an ECOWAS Cultural Framework and WAHO is mirrored by the rhetoric between heads of state in West Africa and the desire by regional leaders to vest decisions on health issues into the hands of those most equipped to deal with regional health issues. For example, during the 1986 Ordinary Meeting of the Authority Heads of State, Carlos Corriea of Guinea-Bissau argued on behalf of moving forward with the merger of the two health organizations, citing the need for "cultural commonalities" and "cooperation across linguistic lines" to make health a part of [economic] integration (ECOWAS 1986). Alhaji Mahama Iddrisu, Minister of Defense of Ghana at the time, also echoed these sentiments, stating "if ECOWAS ever wants to realize its political, economic, and social potential, it is the view of Ghana that any joint efforts between Anglophone and Francophone countries be respective of the unique cultures among us" (ECOWAS 1986).

More importantly, ECOWAS' desire to create a regional health organization based in the embrace of a dynamic West African culture and based on generating technical, West African expertise and health practices is a signal that the Ministers of Health in West Africa did not believe that whatever would come out of the Bamako Initiative would be representative or enough to deal with the full scale of health issues within West Africa. The emergence of WAHO alongside the amako Initiative represents a form of West African agency that can explain the seemingly ineffective practices and embrace of the Bamako Initiative and the basis of regional convergence in the area of health.

Understanding the development of regional health within the first ten years of its existence as mainly a formative embrace of cultural diversity and organizational expansion beyond economic integration sheds light on the emergent practices of regional convergence in the area of public health. Regional convergence understood as the process in which political and social behaviors become constant began with the institutional change of merging the Francophone and Anglophone health organizations and creating the Assembly of Health Ministers as the decision-making and coordinating body of WAHO in 1987. WAHO represented the first instance within ECOWAS where full decision-making authority was not vested only with the Authority Heads of State.[6] This was significant, as it gave the Assembly of Health Ministers autonomy in deciding how to coordinate and harmonize the region when it came to health. The Assembly of Health Ministers would also provide specialized and technical expertise of the health dynamics in their respective member states to develop best practices and the training of health professionals in West Africa.

The progress of the regional health integration process in West Africa would receive its first real test in 1989, with the onset of the Liberian Civil War and Sierra Leone, shortly after. The devastation of these civil wars left in its wake fragile and broken societies faced with crumbling infrastructure and residual effects from the wars, such as internal displacement and the destruction of hospitals and homes, and the inflow of illicit drugs into the region. The most notable confluence of these unfortunate dynamics comes from the use of child soldiers in both Liberia and Sierra Leone. Former child soldiers often recollect on their reliance on drugs to help them fight and feel "fearless." Former female child soldiers also willingly and unwillingly partook in the civil war used drugs and sometimes were sexually assaulted and raped. The aftermath of war brought to bear a new reality in West Africa and an increased justification for a multifaceted approach to health in the region.

When West Africa was embroiled in civil war throughout the 1990s, the region also came into prominence as a hub for illicit drug trafficking, from South America, through West Africa, to Europe. Alongside the emergence of drug trafficking in West Africa was the rise of drug consumption. The increase in drug consumption was symptomatic of the lack of surveillance of the flow of drugs and the need for rural communities, particularly on the borders, to have access to illicit drugs and prescription drugs. With the poorly regulated distribution of drugs in the region came an increase of drug abuse in the region. The presence of war in West Africa also contributes to the porous health dynamic in the region. For instance, in examining HIV prevalence during the civil war in Guinea-Bissau, infectious disease researchers found HIV prevalence to be higher during times of civil war. The reasons for increased HIV prevalence, the authors argue, is that civil conflicts have in some cases been shown to increase the transmission of HIV in societies by mechanisms such as population movements, increase in commercial sexual activities, sexual abuse, transitory sexual relations, as well as the collapse of health structures leading to unsafe injections and blood transfusion routines. Medical centers and health clinics are also vulnerable during times of civil war.[7] Intrastate conflicts challenge neutrality norms and our ability to recognize the dangers of health care delivery in times of conflict.

The enormity and emergence of drug abuse, coupled with the residual effects of civil war, have contributed to a series of transnational health crises in West Africa. The infectious disease and the increase in noncommunicable diseases have contributed to a "disease burden" in the region, with the causes attributed to poor oversight, lifestyle changes, and improper or negligible diagnosis (WHO 2014). From this vantage point, regional stakeholders have worked together to discern a coordinated response to transnational health issues. For instance, at the 15th World Health Assembly in 1997, African health ministers began to frame health as an economic and security issue. This framing has become a consistent part of the narrative of West African Health ministers over the years globally and within the subregion. As such, framing health as a holistic development issue and the provision of health services are therefore strengthened by improved capacity in all development sectors.

WAHO and the ECOWAS Commission: A New Mandate

In examining the institutional development of ECOWAS, that is, how ECOWAS over time has responded to the fluid dynamics of West African society, we can consider two institutional transformations. First is the Revised Treaty of 1993 and the second is the birth of the ECOWAS Commission in 2007.[8] Given the conflict context in the region and the need to improve health research and surveillance competencies across the region, the Authority Heads of State in ECOWAS embedded WAHO fully into the ECOWAS institutional framework in 1998. WAHO explicitly focused on disease as the biggest burden in the region and focused less on capacity and health infrastructure building in its first strategic plan in 2003 (Aidam and Sombié 2016).

WAHO's institutional development gets its shot in the arm during ECOWAS' second transformation. In the period of the first transformation from 1993 to 2007, the Assembly Ministers of Health continued to meet regularly (biannually) and WAHO as a specialized institution of ECOWAS still operated as an aside to the organization, rather than an integrated unit. The lack of integration of WAHO into the strategic vision of ECOWAS during its first transformation is evidenced by its exclusion from any strategic plan of the then ECOWAS Secretariat. Health gets a passive mention as a priority in the post-civil war context in the strategic plans of ECOWAS in 2002–2003, but the strategic plan does not include WAHO in a collaborative manner.

In 2007, the ECOWAS Secretariat became the ECOWAS Commission, changing the organization and institutional structure of ECOWAS and its component pieces.[9] The ECOWAS Commission units responsible for elements of the health agenda are Human Development and Gender and Agriculture, Environment, and Water Resources. The change in institutional structure to the commission also meant an updated mandate for WAHO. Ahead of the shift to the ECOWAS Commission, the Assembly Ministers of Health amended the original protocol establishing the WAHO and its purpose within ECOWAS at the 49th and 50th ordinary meetings. The Assembly Ministers of Health resolved to the following changes to the original mandate of WAHO:

- More decision-making power vested into the Director-General, notably the ability to appoint all staff and officials of WAHO (formerly the duty of Assembly Ministers of Health)
- The creation of four specialized technical divisions embedded in the General Directorate of WAHO: Division of Human Resource Development; Division of Research and Health Management Information Systems; Division of Primary Health Care and Disease Control; Division of Planning and Technical Assistance
- A WAHO-specific budget, approved by the Administrative and Finance Commission of ECOWAS (ECOWAS 2006[10]).

The Assembly of Health Ministers sought to integrate the WAHO mandate into the broader ECOWAS Commission strategy by providing more autonomy to the Director-General to engage in partnerships, pursue relevant health initiatives, and set the strategic course for the organization. In allowing more autonomy to be vested in the Director-General and by increasing the technical capacity of WAHO, the Assembly of Health Ministers helped create a space for practitioners within the Commission and within WAHO to negotiate a more direct and important role for health in ECOWAS, while enhancing WAHO's autonomy as a specialized institution of ECOWAS.

Health-based Community of Practice

In the broader ECOWAS Commission, the Humanitarian and Social Affairs Directorate, which is part of the Social Affairs and Gender Commission, primarily deals with issues related to health. Within the directorate, the Health Programme Development Unit is specifically tasked to work directly with WAHO to implement the ECOWAS Health Development Programme. The Humanitarian and Social Affairs Directorate is also responsible for incorporating risk reduction strategies, including public health outbreaks. Most of the health practitioners here and in WAHO spent at least ten years working in some capacity on regional issues within or on behalf of ECOWAS. The ECOWAS Emergency Response Team (EERT) is also embedded within the Humanitarian and Social Affairs Division. Their mandate is to develop a joint civilian and professional emergency response mechanism that would deploy during peace operations and/or health crises throughout the region. The EERT is run by three officials charged with defining the capacity and targeting recruitment for the EERT. Officials in the Humanitarian and Social Affairs Division and in WAHO point to their experiences working in other international institutions, particularly commenting on the lack of serious attention placed on issues in the subregion as part of their motivation for working in ECOWAS. For example, a coordinator in the Humanitarian and Social Affairs division highlighted how after working for the UN as an international lawyer, they returned to Nigeria to work for ECOWAS because of a desire to work through the organization to amend for the lack of attention to African issues.[11] Practitioners are driven by their desire to enhance and develop the region in a way that privileged African perspectives and expertise. This was also reflected by the former Director General of WAHO, Dr. Xavier Crespin, who in his opening remarks at the 16th Ordinary Meeting of the ECOWAS Council of Health Ministers argued that an essential pillar of socioeconomic development in West Africa is a "healthy population" and suggested that regional health actors take ownership of developing a regional health strategy that is motivated by a desire to impact local communities and build the capacity of member states to manage health crises in their domain (ECOWAS 2015).

As the drivers of regional health convergence, the WAHO community of practice facilitates harmonization of member states and builds standards of behaviors and practices that traverse different scales of governance and permeate throughout the region. In an effort to root regional health governance in a cultural frame unique to the dynamics on the ground, health practitioners engage in two related strategies to network the region. First is the use of MoU to articulate and formalize their relationships with regional stakeholders. Second is using "capacity-building" as a strategy to build best practices, standardize behavior, and build health systems through the community level. Capacity building is also used to assert agency over health matters, as the goal of health-related capacity-building strategy is to create a fiscally self-sustaining regional health infrastructure that is not heavily reliant on external actors. By engaging in these strategies, WAHO practitioners can engage and leverage their autonomy as a specialized organ of ECOWAS. The networks formed through these strategies indicate the institutional space created by ECOWAS in formulating WAHO and the Commission. Further, practitioners are able to eschew resource issues by using these strategic techniques to build financial networks to enhance regional health governance.

Strategizing Harmonization

In building regional health networks, WAHO practitioners focus their networking strategy on the dissemination of health information, health research, the promotion of good health practices, and the development of resources for health medicines, vaccines, and health financing (ECOWAS 2007–2008). These practitioners specifically link the harmonization of regional health policies and standards to ECOWAS' free movement protocols, arguing that harmonization will improve health service provision in ECOWAS member states. Following the reorganization of WAHO, practitioners and health ministers have argued that regional health infrastructure has struggled due to governance issues, inadequate funding, poor coordination between member states in controlling and containing cross-border epidemics, and a short supply of qualified health professionals and medical products.[12] In response to these constraints, practitioners have advocated for policies that enhance the free movement of health resources, implementing increased health budgets, harmonization of disease control, improved flow of health information, and more involvement with private sector health actors.

WAHO practitioners are acutely aware of the immediacy of a regional health institution that can eliminate barriers and obstacles to regional health service delivery and how that may sometimes come into tension with broader institutional goals and the fragility of poorly developed national health systems. For instance, WAHO's institutional priorities were broad in scope—the promotion of health sustainable health policies in West Africa, capacity building and sustainability of WAHO, and strengthening networks with regional health stakeholders. However, as Dr. Carlos Brito, Director of Public Health and Research in the Department of Disease and Epidemic Control underscores, the broad strategic approach limited WAHO's ability to hone in on the priorities of the region, particularly in response to acute public health emergencies. Practitioners like Brito mention that WAHO is not an "implementing body, but a facilitating body" but also mention WAHO's presence and ability to be a first responder at the onset of epidemics in the region. Brito explained how the Ebola crisis led to an expansion and clearer articulation of the strategic focus of WAHO. According to Brito and other practitioners, the Ebola outbreak led to a refocus on the regional capacity to combat recurring epidemics and build sustainable health development. The result is an organizational focus on five thematic areas: (1) Maternal, Child and Adolescent Health; (2) Quality Standards and Centres of Excellence; (3) Pharmaceuticals (medicines and vaccines); (4) Prevention and Control of Communicable and non-Communicable Diseases; and (5) Health Information.[13]

Understanding the strategic goals of WAHO is important to the process of regional integration for three reasons. First, it highlights the strategic and purposeful nature of the networking process in West Africa. Second, it allows ECOWAS/WAHO to identify and specify regional health stakeholders and creates a linkage between ECOWAS, the stakeholders, and a tangible outcome related to public health. Third, the strategic goals over time provide a road map that helps trace the process and progress of regional health practices in West Africa, providing the ability to assess the effectiveness of regional health infrastructure and governance over time.

A part of the harmonization process by ECOWAS/WAHO in health is to develop and incorporate standards that span across the region. For instance, in following the initiative to increase more health professional training and to increase the availability of health professionals in rural societies, practitioners advocated for a standardization of health certificates and diplomas across the region, to ensure that health professional training would be consistent throughout West Africa.[14] This proposed harmonization plan would also consider the creation of medicine registration concentration on a regional scale, creating a larger regional pharmaceutical marketplace for member states and their citizens. However, the realization of such plans faces a hurdle, a lack of consensus in the perceptions of health practitioners.

There are two challenges of harmonization in health practices. First is the perspective that harmonization is indeed necessary; however, it should occur in the context of other social development programs of ECOWAS and not be exclusively a technical project by health officials. Aloize Amechi, head of the EERT, argued for more coordination and integration of WAHO's facilitation efforts with other departments within the commission and explicit linkage between health and humanitarian and political policies of ECOWAS.[15] Another part of the challenge of harmonization is that health interventions from the organization have typically been excluded from ECOWAS' pillars of intervention. As one practitioner who is involved with the WAHO response to Ebola recalled, the responses to epidemics and facilitating the development of national health systems through regional cooperation take time and the communication strategy between WAHO and ECOWAS was difficult to coordinate. Multiple practitioners lamented on the slow movement of the development of the ECOWAS Regional Centre for Surveillance and Disease Control, which was proposed by the Assembly of Health Ministers to the Authority Heads of State in May 2009. An immense number of human lives were lost—over 11,000 from March 2014 to December 2015 in West Africa, which accelerated the ECOWAS RCSDC. The combination of a lack of intraorganizational cooperation and expediency of political actors within ECOWAS, serve as significant hurdles to harmonization.

Practitioners are also aware that they are combating an inherently hierarchical institution, which in many ways constrain their ability to react to epidemics and other public health crises with expedience. According to one practitioner, WAHO is not a "partner" of states and they refer to their "boss" as the Ministers of Health in member states. However, they also recognize that their role is specifically to influence states to adopt and implement decisions and recommendations that come from their domain. In recognizing the hierarchy, practitioners are acutely aware of the need to change or alter their strategies of communication to assure that they are not only maintaining the hierarchy that exists in ECOWAS, more broadly, but also engaging with relevant stakeholders in a manner that incorporates the expertise and interests of practitioners.

Returning to the example of the Ebola response, WAHO was tasked with coordinating and facilitating high-level meetings of ministers of health and foreign affairs ministers from member states. In these series of meetings, which took place in late March 2014, deploying emergency health services and equipment during the Ebola outbreak, WAHO was able to provide 10 million USD to the affected countries (Liberia, Sierra Leone, and Guinea) soon after they made public declarations of the epidemic. Also in their facilitating role, WAHO practitioners were able to help provide health information to Ministers of Health across West Africa, and practitioners were permitted to mobilize resources to further ECOWAS' response to the outbreak. A key part of the harmonizing strategy was to allow the three most affected countries explicitly indicate what their priorities and needs were to mitigate the impact on human lives. However, WAHO's ability to provide these resources to facilitate the process of adopting harmonization strategies in health begins with the creation of three- to five-person teams of ECOWAS practitioners that are responsible for constructing a strategy of harmonization that matches up with the strategic goals of WAHO, identifying regional stakeholders, and engaging member states through national- or local-level interactions.

> All of our frameworks are chosen and developed in consultation with partners. International partners, local authorities, everybody who is considered a stakeholder is carried along. And once there is an agreement as to what goes into the framework, according to our own practice in ECOWAS it has to be adopted by member states.[16]

The role of the small team of ECOWAS practitioners is vital to the process of regional convergence. This team is responsible for developing the linkage of health practices from the bottom-up and also determining what actors are relevant and purposeful in producing regional health policies. These small teams are responsible for consultation, monitoring and evaluation, and program creation and implementation. ECOWAS practitioners go "on the ground" to assess the viability of their organizational goals, while also looking to engage local health stakeholders within member states. Overall, the work of these teams of ECOWAS practitioners has led to the creation of specialized relationships between ECOWAS/WAHO, international organizations, and health NGOs. These relationships are largely due to the technical and organizational expertise of ECOWAS practitioners, as well as their privileging the importance of engagement from member state societies.

ECOWAS and the West African Commission on Drugs: A Multifaceted Partnership

In October 2011, ECOWAS Commission President Kadre Desire Ouedraogo solicited members of the Human Development and Gender Commission, the Director General and Deputy General of WAHO–Dr. Placido Cardoso and Dr. Jeanetta Johnson, respectively, with special consultation from former Nigerian President, Olusegun Obasanjo, to meet and discuss the possibility of ECOWAS constructing a solution to the growing drug problem in West Africa. The reason for the meeting was to discuss an actionable plan from ECOWAS, with the cooperation of experts throughout the reason, to develop a coordinated response to drugs in the region in the same way the region came together to combat small arms in the late 1990s and early 2000s.[17] Sintiki Ugbe, a member of the Humanitarian and Social Division in ECOWAS, says of the initial meeting:

> Ouedraogo, was pretty passive about what he wanted, which is why he brought in Obasanjo. [Obasanjo] is a powerful voice in West Africa, so it was our job to come up with a proposal that dealt with this issue. Drugs came to West Africa because of war. As we move away from war, we had to focus on freeing West Africa from drugs. When we came together, we thought it best to include all stakeholders, rather than include only heads of state. That is why we decided to create WACD.[18]

As a result of this initial meeting, members of the ECOWAS Human Development and Gender Commission as well as President Obasanjo began to recruit health experts and experts on human and drug trafficking and eventually convened the West African Commission on Drugs in January of 2013. ECOWAS, the Kofi Annan Foundation, the African Union (AU), and the UN Office on Drugs and Crime were identified as the key organizational partners in the commission. However, through the suggestions of the ECOWAS Commission and President Obasanjo, the West African Commission on drugs was made up heavily of regional experts and civil society NGOs who provided background knowledge of the drug problem in West Africa. Yande Diop, also an ECOWAS practitioner of Health who worked with West Africa Commission on Drugs (WACD), stated, "we at ECOWAS want to use [WACD] in conjunction with our institutional mandates. The information we gathered from WACD we can use as part of a strategy for ECOWAS"[19] As such, the make of WACD ended up being quite diverse. A ten-person group of representatives from nine of the 15 ECOWAS member states and one representative from Mauritania constituted the heads of the commission:

- Dr. Idrissa Ba, Child psychiatrist and addictologist, Senegal
- Justice Bankole Thompson, Former judge on the Special Court of Sierra Leone

- Dr. Mary Chinery Hesse, member of the AU Panel of the Wise, Ghana
- Dr. Alpha Abdoulaye Diallo, National Coordinator of Réseau Afrique Jeunesse, an NGO focused on Youth engagement and empowerment, Guinea
- Christine Kafando, Founder of Association Espoir pour Demain (AED), a civil society organization aimed at improving the quality of life for women and children, particularly those affected by HIV/AIDS, Burkina Faso
- Edem Kodjo, Former Prime Minister of Togo
- Pedro Pires, Former President of Cabo Verde
- Adeolu Ogunrombi, Project Coordinator for YouthRISE, Nigeria
- Dr. Mohammed Mahmoud Ould Mohamedou, Professor, Graduate Institute of Geneva, Mauritania
- Oumou Sangare, Singer/Songwriter, Mali

During the first commission meeting in Accra Ghana in January 2013, representatives from the United Nations office for Drugs and Crime (UNODC), the European Union delegation to Ghana, the AU, ECOWAS, USAID, Inter-Governmental Action Group against Money Laundering in West Africa (GIABA), the National Drug Law Enforcement Agency of Nigeria, Drug Control Tanzania, and the Global Commission on Drugs worked with members of WACD to help define the vision of the commission and the scope of its regional activities. One of the priorities pushed by ECOWAS was developing a consensus in defining drug use as a public health concern of West Africa and pushing for the decriminalization of drug use. WACD in their inaugural commission report in 2014 declare:

> Cocaine, heroin and ATS have become increasingly available in the region, leading to greater use and dependence, especially among young people. The absence of effective treatment and harm reduction services for people with drug use disorders poses important public health risks, aggravating existing health challenges, including HIV and hepatitis C. The criminalization of all minor drug-related offenses not only places users at greater risk, but also fuels corruption and places an unnecessary burden on already overwhelmed criminal justice systems, and removes the focus from those high-level targets whose activities should be the real target of law enforcement.

Ecorcrats linked the implications of the criminalization of drug use to the increases in human rights violations and imprisonment in member states, urging the UNODC to temper its language linking drug use to terrorism and corruption.[20] WACD decided to intentionally include rhetoric from the Director of the UNODC in justifying classifying drug use as a matter of public health, including in its inaugural report words from Yury Fedorov, director of UNODC in 2013.

> It is important to reaffirm the original spirit of the conventions, focusing on health. The conventions are not about waging a "war on drugs" but about protecting the "health and welfare of mankind."[21]

At the same time ECOWAS practitioners worked to have international organizations frame drug use as a public health problem, they also used the commission and its members to gather information on the health dynamics in member states to craft a regional strategy, through WAHO, to increase health promotion within the region. Citing low levels of inclusion on the social determinants of health in determining the effectiveness of health programs, ECOWAS practitioners from the Humanitarian and Social Affairs Division of the ECOWAS Commission believed it was important to incorporate discussions of the implications of drug use into discussions of how to strengthen member state's capacity for integrating health promotion into development policies. The efforts of ECOWAS practitioners to incorporate drug use into health and development strategy in WAHO manifest itself as a strategic goal in WAHO, starting from 2013 up through the strategic vision of WAHO in 2020. A primary objective of the strategic goal of incorporating social determinants of health in increasing the promotion and effectiveness of health programs in West Africa is to change the behavior of citizens—meaning WAHO programs and interventions were to change the perceptions West Africans as a whole had on access to health programs, the role of traditional medicine, and to move past self-medication as a treatment. A shift in behavior also meant that local and national development policies included explicit mentions of drug use as a public health problem.

While the codified strategic plans, intentions, and initiatives of WAHO and WACD provide a necessary contextualizing of the link between public health, drug use, and the effects on development, the role of ECOWAS practitioners in constructing strategies and messaging on the global and local levels simultaneously is important in the context of convergence for two reasons. First, understanding convergence as a process of shaping modes of behavior, ECOWAS practitioners quite explicitly develop a strategy that directly aims to change the modes of behavior on multiple scales of governance. Second, the capacity for ECOWAS practitioners to network the region through WACD minimizes the perception that one actor is responsible for changing governance in West Africa. More importantly, the manner in which ECOWAS practitioners incorporate multiple actors and stakeholders to create and sustain WACD indicates a cognizance that regional health infrastructure ought to (in a normative sense) be inclusive of all members and actors in society, delimiting the idea that regional governance, particularly in the realm of health, is a state-dependent project.

WAHO and CORDS: Convergence Through MoUs

The Ebola Virus Outbreak in 2014, which directly affected six West African states (Sierra Leone, Liberia, Guinea, Nigeria, Senegal, and Mali) highlighted the lack of emergency preparedness on all scales of governance—from local to international. There was a variation of response to Ebola within the region as well, as Nigeria and Senegal were first to be declared "Ebola-free" in 93 days. Conversely, it took over a year for Sierra Leone, Liberia, and Guinea to be declared "Ebola-free." ECOWAS/WAHO was heavily criticized for its response to Ebola, as the United States and the AU were considered to be more active in quelling Ebola. The Ebola Crisis of 2014–2016 was significant primarily because it was the first time Ebola had spread to an urban area. The response to Ebola came primarily from the African Union, the United States, financial support from the European Union, health workers from the affected countries.[22]

ECOWAS was noticeably absent from any coordinated effort to quell Ebola at its onset and at the height of the outbreak. However, ECOWAS convened an extraordinary session in October 2014 to develop a strategy of how to engage the organization in the fight against Ebola. It was at this session, amongst the Authority Heads of State where the Human Development and Gender, Dr. Fatimata Dia Sow argued that ECOWAS and WAHO would need to create a mechanism for response to health crises and improve the capacity of the EERT to also be expanded into the realm of health. The ECOWAS Commission and WAHO advocated and received 2.6 million USD to provide surveillance and health supplies to member states to manage the outbreak. Guinea, Liberia, and Sierra Leone received the bulk of the financial support from WAHO.

Understanding the need for a preventative approach to future emergency health outbreaks, in September 2015, Dr. Sow tasked the Humanitarian and Social Affairs Division and the ECOWAS Gender Development Division coordinators to work with WAHO to establish partnerships around the region aimed at improving the EERT and partnerships that would develop a capacity for member states to better survey the prospects of communicable diseases ravishing the region. Three gender development officials and one official from Humanitarian and Social Affairs made up the delegation that worked with WAHO officials in the Division of Research and Health Management Information Systems. The combined group of ECOWAS and WAHO officials decided that any partnership would aid in the development of a regional center for disease control and surveillance and the establishment of a Network for Epidemiological Surveillance and Communicable Disease Control as approved by the Assembly Ministers of Health in 2013. Part of the strategy of ECOWAS/WAHO on finding partners was to rely upon existing structures within and outside the region, rather than creating the parameters for a regional disease control mechanism from the ground up. ECOWAS/WAHO also focused specifically on expertise, knowledge production, and capacity building as pillars for the prospective partnership, rather than financial, as the goal of the group was to develop an actionable mechanism for outbreak prevention.

ECOWAS/WAHO sought the expertise and partnership of Connecting Organizations for Regional Disease Surveillance (CORDS) in late October

2015. CORDS is an organization focused on facilitating disease information exchange and communication exchange among various networks in South East Asia, East Africa, South East Europe, Southern Africa, the Mekong Basin, and the Middle East. Through the facilitation of information, CORDS is able to make "vital contributions to national emergency response planning leveraging knowledge of disease outbreaks around the globe."[23] CORDS already had a footprint on the African Continent, with networks such as Southern African Centre for Infectious Disease Surveillance (SACIDS) and the East African Integrated Disease Network (EAIDSnet). These established networks are mostly responsible for providing research, enhancing health professional training, and improving data sharing.

The Project Director of CORDS, Dr. Bakary Sylla, and the Project Management Consultant, Ms Emma Orefuwa, suggested a "Champions" meeting, which took place in Dakar, Senegal, in November 2015, which brought together ECOWAS/WAHO and CORDS and related stakeholders to discuss the possibilities of creating a regional network for infectious disease surveillance. Representatives from SACIDS and EAIDSnet came to the Champions meeting to share their experiences of networking with CORDS and how the relationships between the subregions and CORDS have helped improve regional health dynamics. After the Champions meeting, ECOWAS practitioners met twice with CORDS in December 2015 and January, officials from SACIDS and EAIDSnet, as well as Emma Orefuwa to begin drafting an MoU with CORDS.

Abimbola Oyehunnu of ECOWAS' Humanitarian and Social Affairs Unit describes the drafting of the WAHO/CORDS MoU as a "mutually beneficial and productive" process. In drafting the MoU, the goal of both WAHO and CORDS was to increase the standards and practices of health professionals and improve the spread of information about infectious diseases in West Africa. ECOWAS practitioners pushed for sharing data on public health, because to this point, information sharing was not a common practice in the region, though WAHO had identified its desire to share data on infectious diseases in its 2009–2013 strategic agenda. In working with CORDS, ECOWAS practitioners pushed for the MoU to justify to member states how data sharing is linked to harmonization. For instance, ECOWAS practitioners discussed linking the role of public health and information sharing as a necessary component of achieving the sustainable development goals.[24] ECOWAS practitioners pushed for the creation of a variant to a national center of excellence in each member state, which would end up in the MoU as "National Coordination Institutes," which would serve as the information clearing house for a proposed West African Network for Infectious Disease Surveillance (WANIDS). WANIDS would then be embedded within the ECOWAS Regional Centre for Surveillance and Disease Control (ECOWAS-RCSDC). CORDS would have autonomy over the operationalization of WANIDS, while ECOWAS/WAHO would provide support to WANIDS by mobilizing efforts in the member states and benefit from an existing information database that would be used in the EERT as well as a prospective infectious disease early warning directorate, which would be a part of ECOWAS-RCSDC. The MoU between WAHO and CORDS came into force on February 10, 2016.

On the surface, the MoU between CORDS and WAHO appears to be a mutually beneficial and strategic partnership. The negotiation process resulted in very little contentious argumentation; however, understanding the process and substance of argumentation allows for the examination of meaning behind harmonization practices. For example, we can understand the practice of information sharing as more that of a utility for quelling the spread of infectious disease. We can understand the sharing of data as a practice that builds trust throughout the region. By creating a standard of information sharing through embedding mechanisms on the national level, ECOWAS practitioners and CORDS members alike demonstrate the value of shifting behavior modes for health practitioners in West Africa.

While the use of the MoU in some regards is to formalize partnerships, the role of the MoU in shaping the partnerships between ECOWAS and other regional actors is also communicative. That is, ECOWAS in this case not only uses the MoU to assert the nature of its partnership and its utility but also uses the MoU as a way to transmit its messages, policies, and normative ideas through informal actors in the region. The MoU between WAHO and CORDS helps solve some of ECOWAS' implementation issues in the development of health information systems, but the MoU is also sending a signal that there are incentives and benefits to harmonization and that the message of harmonization can and should come from other actors who may be more in tune with the dynamics embedded in individual member states. In a more direct manner, the MoU between WAHO and CORDS also gives weight to the rhetorical aims of each institution.

Convergence Through Capacity Building

Woven through the numerous policy documents, strategic plans, and memorandums on public health in West Africa is the persistent claim of the need for regional institutional capacity building and capacity building on the local and national levels in order to realize the potential of regional health governance fully. ECOWAS practitioners interpret capacity building to mean "the ability for ECOWAS member states to accomplish their goals by identifying their needs, sources of support, and the ability to have adequate structures to reach their goals."[25] When asked to identify the hurdles to health governance in West Africa, ECOWAS practitioners overwhelmingly answered weak/poor health systems and a lack of capacity on the member states' level.

Suppose one is to interpret the definition of capacity building offered by various ECOWAS practitioners. In that case, it could be argued and maintained that a notion of capacity building that relies on the functioning of structures is vulnerable to a functionalist idea of capacity building—that is, the idea that regional governance can only survive based on the strong functioning of its institutions. If these structures are inherently weak, then the project of regional health governance is inherently limited. However, a proper understanding of ECOWAS practitioners and their desire to include capacity building as a core feature of regional health convergence indicates a desire of ECOWAS practitioners and West Africans to affect regional change themselves. Thus, asserting that member states can accomplish and identify their needs and sources of support indicates that there is less of an understanding of what capacity building is, but a better, practical understanding of how to build capacity:

> For me, as they say experience is the best teacher. ECOWAS has been for over 40 years now. In addition, I believe that is a reflection of where we are coming from, which is driving the current state. A lot of resources were pumped into maintaining territorial integrity, peace, security, forgetting the people who actually bear the brunt of crisis. So now you can say there is a shift to what taking care of the people. Because you realize it is the people who [inaudible], so I believe that it is the experience that our past leaders had that made them refocus from an ECOWAS of States to an ECOWAS of people. So you will see that most of the laws and policies focus on people now.[26]
>
> In regards to capacity building … [A] lot of tools have been developed that can be used to help member states, directly, so now the engagement is deeper and it has moved from the surface to down touching the people directly. From the peace and security perspective, you can see that there are things that are done to make sure there is some stability. Recovery, for example when there is a humanitarian crisis and those things are centered on livelihood, supporting women and children, an capacity building for youth entrepreneurship. The vision like I said before is based on the people and the future. The future for this region depends on the capacities of the people who make up the region, community citizens themselves.[27]

Capacity building manifests itself in the realm of regional health governance in three ways. First, in WAHO, practitioners have created strategies and policies that put health governance back in the hands of the people. Second, ECOWAS practitioners have pushed for health to be considered alongside broader regional harmonization efforts. Third, ECOWAS practitioners have pushed for public health to become a part of the human rights agenda for ECOWAS, particularly in building up the EERT's civil deployment provision.

Part of WAHO's attempt at capacity building is to create practices that build the health institutions on the local and national level. For example, the previously mentioned MoU with CORDS creates national centers for the dissemination of health research and health surveillance. In addition to this practice, WAHO has also pushed for health workers within member states to send real-time reports to develop a more robust health analysis system. Specifically, WAHO created an epidemic-prone bulletin that would be disseminated to all health divisions of member states, and built the health data management capacity in Burkina Faso, Ghana, Guinea-Bissau, Nigeria, and Senegal by providing the health ministries in these countries with technology to supplement their existing warehouse structures for data management. WAHO also provided $100,000 to Niger and Togo to develop and implement their strategic health research development plans and provided support to the West African Health Research Network (WAHRNET) that led to the publication of the West African Health Research Journal (ECOWAS/WAHO 2014).

It is also a common sentiment among ECOWAS practitioners to stress the lack of intraorganizational harmonization efforts. A common argument for capacity building was the insistence that public health be integrated into broader regional frameworks. For example, ECOWAS practitioners used ECOWAS' visa-less travel policy and the protocol on the free movement of people to justify the need for the free movement of health professionals throughout the region. WAHO stressed in its strategic vision the need to build and improve the pharmaceutical industry in West Africa:

> Deepen reflections on the issue of tariff to be applied to medicines to protect the regional pharmaceutical industry within the ECOWAS Common External Tariff framework. (propose to the Directorate of Customs relative to medicines and raw materials for the manufacturing of medicines that ought to either enjoy tax imposition or waivers within the framework of a single taxation regime in the ECOWAS countries)
>
> (WAHO 2014)

Similarly, WAHO has suggested that there should also be convergence between ECOWAS' labor policies and public health. The benefits of such practices move ECOWAS away from practicing and achieving public health outcomes that are dependent solely on state interventions and constraints of not having the best health professionals, technology, or materials at one's disposal. ECOWAS practitioners believe that capacity building in this regard can help West Africans obtain the same types and quality of health care no matter where they go in the region.

An apparent method of inciting regional convergence in public health is defining public health in a manner that becomes relevant for other actors and regional stakeholders. To make public health more Afro-centric and region-specific, WAHO used a development frame to regionalize public health. Similarly, ECOWAS practitioners believe that public health should also become an issue of human rights. Aloize Amechi, head of EERT, argued specifically for public health to become embedded in the EERT response team and that health workers should play a pivotal role in any response to regional health crises:

In order to build capacity for member states to incorporate public health into the human rights agenda, Amechi in his capacity of Head Humanitarian Officer of the EERT offers the creation of an emergency civil deployment unit by establishing a Civilian Humanitarian Standby Roster to complement an emergency peace and security standby roster. The goal of the Civilian Humanitarian Standby Roster as it pertains to public health capacity building is to create a database of deployable West African Health experts to assess the livelihood of those who dwell in Refugee/IDP camps, the water and sanitation conditions, child and gender protections, nutritionists, the prospects for epidemics, and psycho-social trauma of civilians during an emergency. These experts will be trained for a year on how to include their best practices in emergency situations (deemed in this case, issues of peace and security). The experts can be deployed for six months after the end of the training. By embedding these experts as part of the emergency response mechanism in ECOWAS, the EERT creates an institutional capacity for public health to be incorporated into more than just the training and building of health information systems and health services. Conceiving public health as a human rights concern in the region stratifies the importance of regional health governance and the multifaceted ways in which health governance matters to the regionalization process.

Conclusion

While ECOWAS is known mainly for its expansive peace and security architecture, regional health governance has emerged over the years as an area of high importance. Though the Ebola Virus crisis brought health issues to the forefront in ECOWAS, the process of regional convergence in health has been a priority for the organization. ECOWAS practitioners of public health engage in various networking techniques, primarily using MoUs, institutional capacity building, and incorporating civil society and multiple regional health stakeholders into the convergence process.

ECOWAS' strategy of harmonizing regional health governance deviates from conventional modes of decision-making processes in public health. For instance, some responses and approaches to infectious disease issues worldwide are highly centralized and rely on the capacities and agendas of state-led and/or hierarchal international organizations who prescribe interventions and reproduce power gaps between the global and the local (Riggirozzi and Yeates 2015). Additionally, top-down public health frameworks often push particular norms and practical responses to public health crises that lack the proper regional contexts to pursue "best practices." For example, the global response to Ebola in West Africa highlighted the limits of a state-driven and global institution–driven health policy and found a lack of understanding about the local contexts that exacerbated the crises.

Understanding regional convergence in public health as a process of harmonizing modes of behavior in West Africa is to understand the process of framing the importance of public health practices and how they are embedded in the local levels of governance. ECOWAS practitioners, recognizing the importance of creating health practices that have an immediate impact on the citizens of West Africa, have engaged in networking that connects ECOWAS to other IGOs simultaneously with civil society and local actors. In doing so, ECOWAS is able to act as a unified body and create regional normative frameworks that structure practices in support of social policies and governance, while also creating opportunities for the allocation of resources within the regional space (Riggirozzi 2015, 416; Riggirozzi and Yeates 2015, 222). Through its practices, ECOWAS provides an arena for all regional health stakeholders to collaborate and enhance the effectiveness of health practices and health systems in the region.

One of the implications of ECOWAS' practices of harmonization in public health is the perception that health is still a specialized, technical area and that public health be relegated only to human development and gender within ECOWAS. While ECOWAS practitioners have tried to frame public health as a development and human rights issue, in practice, these frames have only manifested themselves in the health domain. For example, there is hardly a mention of public health development in the Political Affairs or Trade and Customs Commissions of ECOWAS. However, ECOWAS practitioners have stressed the importance of creating a broader organizational appeal to public health as an area of importance in ECOWAS.

ECOWAS practitioners' perceptions of the role of public health in the region prove to be vital to the process of regional health convergence in West Africa. Because of this reality, regional convergence must also account for the cultural contexts of member states and their capacity to build their own viable health systems. ECOWAS has long known the importance of cultural contexts since its inception, which also explains why the discussion and creation of WAHO preceded the Bamako Initiative. As conceived by ECOWAS practitioners, regional convergence derives from a desire for regional actors to create spheres of governance that deepen engagement among peers.

As ECOWAS' regional health infrastructure grows, one can point to the networks and strategies created and pursued by ECOWAS practitioners to highlight regional health governance drivers and trace regional health practices' development over time. Identifying ECOWAS practitioners as the drivers of regional health governance takes the focus away from the state and/or global structures in measuring the effects of health governance and emphasizes the processes of health network formation and the framing of regional health governance to measure the emergence of social and political practices related to health. In a broader context, ECOWAS practitioners and their process-driven network formation and capacity-building strategies offer important insights on the importance of the region in the context of global south regionalisms. The perspective offered here demonstrates the modes of agency and autonomy global south regional organizations can have independent from their constitutive member state governments and stratifies the importance of regional stakeholders and their impact on regional health governance. For example, the ECOWAS-RCDCS would be an imagined idea if not for the partnership between ECOWAS and CORDS. Examining convergence through the activities of ECOWAS practitioners (and other global south regional organization bureaucrats) provides a glimpse as to how regional organizations become reflective of their regional dynamics and strategically build networks across scales to affect change in the region.

Notes

1 Throughout the chapter, I refer to "health infrastructure" using a combination of the United States Department of Health and World Health Organization's definition of public health infrastructure, which is "the capacity to prevent disease, promote health, and prepare for and respond to both acute (emergency) threats and chronic (ongoing) challenges to health." Health infrastructure comprises the institutions, capacity, knowledge and commodities that support public health. For more, see John Powles and Flavio Comim "Public Health Infrastructure and Knowledge", in Smith, Richard, Robert Beaglehole, David Woodward, and Nick Drager (eds.) *Global Public Goods for Health: Health Economics and Public Health Pespectives*, Oxford: Oxford University Press.

2 This is a sentiment shared by Riggirozzi and Yeates (2015), who also argue that the area of health provides a sector-specific lens to examine how Southern regional formations engage in power constellations, institutions, and ideological positions affecting health at different levels of governance.

3 Anonymous, Interview, October 14, 2016, Abuja Nigeria.

4 Anonymous, Interview, October 13, 2016, ECOWAS Secretariat Annex, Abuja Nigeria.

5 This is an important point in understanding the fundamental problems with the Bamako Initiative—particularly when it came to abolishing user fees. According to WAHO officials, people had difficulty determining if they were eligible for certain services because it was not made clear to them by programs in their community. Also, scarcity and the lack of trust also led to community apathy. Most people would refuse to use services or report illnesses, relying on home remedies to cure their ailments.

6 It should also be of note that there was no codified mode of decision-making in ECOWAS prior to the 1993 Revised Treaty. Decisions were often made by simple majority and/or consensus among the Authority Heads of State.

7 There are human rights debates that question whether there are times where norms of medical neutrality apply to times of war. For more, see: Medical Neutrality Protection Act 2013.

8 The first transformation is explained in greater detail in Chapter 3. For the sake of brevity, the first transformation of ECOWAS explicitly expanded the organization beyond its mandate for economic integration and articulated its political and social mandate.

9 For more on the organizational transformation into the ECOWAS Commission, see Chapter 3.

10 Supplementary Protocol Establishing WAHO.

11 Interview, Programme Officer, Humanitarian and Social Affairs, ECOWAS Commission, Abuja, October 2016.

12 Interview, Anonymous ECOWAS Member State Health Liaison, Abuja, August 2019.

13 Interview, Dr. Carlos Brito, WAHO Secretariat, Bobo-Dioulasso, Burkina Faso, August 2019.
14 Interview, Anonymous health official, ECOWAS Commission, Abuja, Nigeria, October 2016.
15 Interview, Alozie Amechi, ECOWAS Commission, Abuja, Nigeria, October 2016.
16 Abimbola Oyehunnu, Interview, October 26, 2016, Abuja Nigeria.
17 The reference to small arms harmonization refers to two protocols that delimit the spread of small arms in West Africa. The first is the Declaration of a Moratorium on Importation, Exportation and Manufacture.
18 Sintiki Ugbe, Interview, October 23, 2016, Abuja, Nigeria.
19 Yande Diop, Interview, October 23, 2016, Abuja, Nigeria.
20 Sinitiki Ugbe, Interview, October 23, 2016, Abuja Nigeria.
21 Contribution of the Executive Director of the United Nations Office on Drugs and Crime to the high-level review of the implementation of the Political Declaration and Plan of Action on International Cooperation toward an Integrated and Balanced Strategy to Counter the World Drug Problem, to be conducted by the Commission on Narcotic Drugs in 2014.
22 Interview, former US Ambassador to the African Union, Reuben Brigety, George Washington University, September 19, 2015.
23 For more information regarding the work of CORDS, see: www.cordsnetwork.org/about-cords/.
24 Abimbola Oyehunnu, Interview, October 26, 2016, Abuja Nigeria.
25 I came to this definition as a synthesis of various answers provided to me during my interviews with health ECOWAS practitioners as well as ECOWAS practitioners in peace and security.
26 Abimbola Oyehunnu, Interview, October 26, 2016 Abuja Nigeria.
27 Sinitike Ugbe, Interview, October 26, 2016, Abuja Nigeria.

References

Aidam, Jude, and Issiaka Sombié. 2016. "The West African Health Organization's Experience in Improving the Health Research Environment in the ECOWAS Region." Health Research Policy and Systems 14(1): Article 30. DOI: 10.1186/s12961-016-0102-7

Benton, Adia. (2014). "The Epidemic Will be Militarized: Watching Outbreak as the West African Ebola Epidemic Unfolds." Available at: https://culanth.org/fieldsights/599-the-epidemic-will-be-militarized-watching-outbreak-as-the-west-african-ebola-epidemic-unfolds.

Benton, Adia, and Kim Yi Dionne. (2015). "International Political Economy and the 2014 West African Ebola Outbreak." African Studies Review 58(01): 223–236. DOI: 10.1017/asr.2015.11

Benton, Adia, and Sa'ed Atshan. (2016). "'Even War has Rules': On Medical Neutrality and Legitimate Non-violence." Culture, Medicine and Psychiatry 40(2): 151–158. Springer. DOI: 10.1007/s11013-016-9491-x

Chukwuani, Chinyere M, Akindeji Olugboji, and Emmanuel Ugbene. (2006). "Improving Access to Essential Drugs for Rural Communities in Nigeria: The Bamako Initiative Re-Visited." Pharmacy World and Science 28(2): 91–95. DOI: 10.1007/s11096-006-9010-1

Dodgson, Richard, and Kelley Lee. (2002). "Global Health Governance: A Conceptual Review." In Global Governance: Critical Perspectives, eds. Rorden Wilkinson and Steve Hughes. London: Routledge, 92–110.

Gnawali, Devendra Prasad, Subhash Pokhrel, Ali Sié, et al. (2009). "The Effect of Community-based Health Insurance on the Utilization of Modern Health Care Services: Evidence from Burkina Faso." Health Policy 90(2–3): 214–222. DOI: 10.1016/j.healthpol.2008.09.015

Nyonator, Frank K., J. Koku Awoonor-Williams, James F. Phillips, et al. (2005). "The Ghana Community-based Health Planning and Services Initiative for Scaling Up Service Delivery Innovation." Health Policy and Planning 20(1): 25–34. DOI: 10.1093/heapol/czi003

Ridde, Valéry. (2011). "Is the Bamako Initiative Still Relevant for West African Health Systems?" International Journal of Health Services: Planning, Administration, Evaluation 41(1): 175–184. DOI: 10.2190/HS.41.1.l

Riggirozzi, Pia, and Nicola Yeates. (2015). "Locating Regional Health Policy: Institutions, Politics, and Practices." Global Social Policy 15(3): 212–228. DOI: 10.1177/1468018115599819

Rock, Joeva, and Foreign Policy in Focus. (2014). "Why Are We Sending Soldiers Trained for War to Respond to the Ebola Crisis?" Available at: www.thenation.com/article/militarizing-ebola-crisis/.

5 Regional Convergence in Finance

The financial system in West Africa, dominated by the banking sector, is experiencing new transnational banking groups and microfinance institutions (MFIs), resulting in pockets of vulnerability in the public banking sector. The emergence of transnational banking groups and MFIs impacts regional financial development in two transformative ways. First, the emergence of new banking groups and MFIs highlights the interbank system's shallow nature in the region, increasing exposure of banks to sovereigns.[1] Second, the capitalized nature of transnational banking groups and MFIs creates the prospect for greater forms of financial inclusion with the reduction of obstacles in the access to finance, which is important in a highly migratory region such as West Africa.

In the last 25 years, regional banks in West Africa have expanded beyond borders in response to economic reforms and declining opportunities at home (Boone 2005; Iheduru 2012; Lewis and Stein 1997; Reinhart and Tokalidis 2003). As such, transnational banking groups and MFIshave transformed the role of public sector and central banking supervisory and regulatory authority. MFIs are able to exercise control over branch and subsidiary banks across the region. West African financial markets have also become increasingly pan-regional, and private equity houses, transnational banking groups, and MFIs have played an important role in building compelling strategic logics to regional buyers and entrepreneurs looking to gain a foothold in Africa's markets. Value creation and organic revenue growth in West African financial markets have materialized by implementing new procedures and processes by transnational banking groups and private equity houses to improve financial governance (Babarinde 2012; Hearn 2011). What has emerged is creating a financial network between transnational banks, MFIs, and private equity firms that have an overt "region-centered" orientation and a financial regulatory authority ceded to non-state business actors (Iheduru 2012, 277).

This chapter examines the process of regional financial convergence in West Africa, which I define through the practices and interactions of bureaucratic actors within ECOWAS that facilitate, network, and normalize regional activities related to finance. The chapter examines the practice of member state financial deregulation and its impact on ECOWAS' move toward transnational

DOI: 10.4324/9780429436734-5

banking and private equity as main methods of accessing capital in West Africa. Deregulation in this context relates to not only financial deregulation but also the overall reduction and decentralization of the state's administrative capacity. The chapter focuses on ECOWAS' engagement in public–private partnerships' and the practice of deregulation, which contributes to the development of regional financial convergence. Regional financial convergence is focused on the interactions between ECOWAS, regional financial institutions, and private businesses. Understanding how ECOWAS and non-state business actors interact provides an important glimpse into the process of how ECOWAS institutionalizes financial practices that shape regional financial governance and regulatory authority within the region.

In identifying the modes of interaction between ECOWAS and non-state business actors, this chapter looks specifically at the ECOWAS Bank of Investment and Development (EBID), a specialized financial organ of ECOWAS, and how its bureaucrats broker ties with transnational financial groups, such as EcoBank transnational banking group and Stanbic-Investment Banking and Trust Company (IBTC) transnational banking group, and their microfinance subsidiaries contribute to the financialization of West Africa. Financialization is defined as the increasing importance of financial markets, financial motives, financial institutions, and financial elites in the operation of the economy and its governing institutions at the local and national levels (Epstein 2005). The networked nature of these financial actors creates a regional regulatory authority and facilitates the ease of business in the region. This chapter interrogates how ECOWAS member states converged on the practice of financial deregulation, thus providing the space for non-state business actors to emerge and network with ECOWAS in the region. The chapter focuses on the extent to which non-state business actors develop and articulate "region-centrality" as the centerpiece of their investment decisions and identifies how the structures, institutional knowledge, and decisions of ECOWAS practitioners in the EBID drive regional convergence. The chapter demonstrates how the regional activity of non-state financial firms leads to a form of regulatory regionalism, demonstrated by ECOWAS' institutionalization of private sector promotion and the institutionalization of the ECOWAS business forum—a network composed mostly of non-state financial actors.

While the contours of corporate governance structures, state-society interactions, colonial vestiges, and business-led development might look similar in other regions, the practice of deregulation in ECOWAS member states and the prevalence of non-state business actors distinguish West Africa from other regions. Conventionally, financial analysis in Africa focuses on the weakness of state institutions, high levels of inequality, and rampant patrimonialism and corruption. However, the story of regional convergence in West Africa puts the emphasis on a different set of actors, redefines the scope and scale in which financial discourses on Africa take place, and highlights the role identity plays in the financialization of the region, providing an alternative lens in which to examine the dynamics of cooperation and institutionalization in West Africa. The chapter examines how ECOWAS has made West Africa more visible for global integration and coordination through the emergence of banking and financial services rather than the sectors traditionally privileged in studies of economic integration.

The aim of this chapter is twofold. The first is to highlight the extent to which the emergence of financialization has connected West Africa. Examining the impact of financialization on regional convergence offers an alternative explanation to how West Africans access capital. The second aim of this chapter is to demonstrate how the interactions between private sector actors and ECOWAS contribute to financialization within ECOWAS while simultaneously producing a conception of regional regulatory authority that brings together the region and distinguishes the nature of financial governance in West Africa. Rather than focusing on the depth and intensity of intraregional trade, a focus on financialization as a mode of regional integration considers how ECOWAS and financial actors in West Africa are engaged in a process of creating and negotiating a set of common rules that promote "public interest" and resolve the "coordination dilemma" (for research on these coordination issues, see: Moravcsik 1998; Pollack 1997, 2003; Mattli 1999; Hix 2013). Regional convergence occurs through the coordinated networking and harmonization practices of ECOWAS bureaucrats who seek to eschew issues of coordination by member states by involving private and commercial actors in the creation of the common rules around access to capital. These interactions help mold the complexion of regulatory regionalism. Put differently, national interest or a lack of political will does not drive the financialization in West Africa. Rather, the interaction between ECOWAS and its non-state business actors causes the move toward financialization and produces practices, such as deregulation, that are not merely legal or enforced structures, but practices that become "disciplining norms and social conventions" of West Africa.[2] Highlighting the networked nature of regional convergence in finance is important in understanding the shift in West Africa from a financial sector based on hierarchy and markets to networks that develop social logics of institutional norms that become prevalent and institutionalized over time.

Regional convergence in finance in West Africa emphasizes less of a state-centric approach and explains the roles identity and networking play in bringing the region together. Perhaps the most notable example of an individual who embodies this idea is Nigerian billionaire Tony Elumelu. The Tony Elumelu Foundation calls itself a Pan-African organization, rooted in collective action, self-determination, and inclusivity. Ecobank is another example of this, as it markets itself as "The Pan-African bank" that "contributes to the integration and socioeconomic development of [West Africa]" with strategies focused on "diaspora services" and creating a "Pan-African presence." Stanbic-IBTC, though tied to the Standard Bank (a Western-based commercial banking entity), developed a corporate social investment strategy that specifically focuses on the health, education, and economic empowerment of West African youth and family—evidenced by its recent contributions of N1.5 million in educational trust funds and prostheses for a family with children born without limbs in Western Nigeria.[3] African Capital Alliance, a private equity firm also markets itself as a "leading Pan-African investment firm" with an international structure and local expertise, an appeal to both global and regional actors.

The scope of these financial actors becomes even more important when considering the progress, or lack thereof, of a West African regional currency. As will be discussed later in the chapter, ECOWAS has struggled with the harmonization of macroeconomic policies, namely, in the single currency. Harmonization on a single currency has also sparked political tensions, evidenced by the usurping of the "Eco" single currency project by French speaking West African countries in late 2019. Similarly, the African Continental Free Trade Agreement (AfCFTA) also poses questions about the motivations and challenges countries will face in determining their ability to integrate their markets fully. Examining the interactions and identity-based nature of private financial actors offers a way to look at the multiple forms of connectivity in the region without privileging formal modes of integration such as formal trade agreements or common currency projects.

A key to understanding regional convergence's conceptual and theoretical approaches is to separate it from the traditional dynamics that do not capture the African context. The emphasis on the practice of deregulation focuses on how the region becomes conducive to financialization. This chapter does not make the argument that the practice of deregulation and deregulation leads to economic growth; rather, it demonstrates the growing importance of the financial sector in ECOWAS through the interactions between ECOWAS and private business actors.

The chapter is divided into three parts. The chapter examines conceptual approaches to regional convergence on finance, namely, hierarchal capitalism and the Varieties of Capitalism (VoC) to contrast with the concept of Africapitalism and more region-based ideas of finance. Hierarchal capitalism and VoC are points of departure mainly to highlight the mechanisms used to assess convergence drivers: diversified business groups, multinational corporations, atomistic labor relations. The chapter also provides an overview of the market conditions (a feature of hierarchal capitalism and VoC) in ECOWAS to emphasize how access to capital in West Africa is not predicated on the strength of the labor market and also to provide a context that foreshadows the domestic conditions that lead to financial deregulation as a strategy for ECOWAS member states.[4] The chapter then highlights the practice of financial deregulation as a mechanism for regional convergence in West Africa. It tethers it to the rise of financialization within the region, resulting in a new form of regulatory regionalism, as part of the convergence process. This part of the chapter also shows how ECOWAS practitioners viewed deregulation and financialization as an opening to facilitate regional convergence in member states through the creation of ECOWAS Business Incubator for

African Women Entrepreneurs (BIAWE) and ends with finacialization's implications on regionalism.

Hierarchal Capitalism

Ben Ross Schneider (2009; 2014) popularized the terms "Hierarchical Capitalism" and "Hierarchical Market Economies (HME)" when referring to the characteristics, organization, and building of firms in Latin America. Schneider claims that in practice, market-oriented reforms in Latin America during the 1980s and 1990s were a business-led development, not a state-led or market-led development (Schneider 2009, 555). For this reason, the VoC emphasis on a "firm's eye view" provides a more accurate depiction of the capitalist dynamics in Latin America.[5] The core features of HMEs in Latin America are diversified business groups, multinational corporations, atomistic labor relations, and low skills. Family-owned and -controlled diversified business groups were typically part of the large domestic firm structure. Schneider's stresses that HMEs are distinct because of the levels of interaction that constitute and develop hierarchical relations between the economies in the region. Schneider characterizes capitalism in Latin America as a region filled with weak and missing institutions but questions how firms respond to weak or absent institutions. Hierarchy or hierarchical relations, according to Schneider, characterize how "people power" is significantly weak. For instance, in Latin America, unions have little influence of hierarchies within a firm because so few workers are able to unionize, file grievances, or have a voice because workers rotate quickly through firms (Schneider 2014, 7).

Schneider's concept of HMEs is one of the few systematic attempts at examining the nature of capitalism in developing countries. In order for one to understand capitalism in this specific context, one needs to understand what facilitates the allocation of resources and specific institutional complementarities that generate a competitive advantage. For Schneider, the power of business in relation to the power of labor is reinforced by the fact that business groups in the region are structured hierarchically and are family-owned and run. Multinational corporations take advantage of low-skilled labor in the manufacturing and tradable sectors, which incentivize business groups to demand low-skilled labor, decreasing the incentive for business groups to invest in high technology reinforce this dynamic. The consequence is that foreign direct investment produces a crowding out effect to national businesses, relegating national and local businesses to low-technology sectors, and there is very little demand for research and development/high-skill labor in the region.

Schneider's hierarchal capitalism argument is relevant to the case of ECOWAS in that it emphasizes the importance of social interactions that create incentive structures to facilitate the ease of business. Schneider also examines what we can call non-state business actors as the conduits of investment decisions and shapers of regional business governance. Although

Schneider's approach does provide a unique perspective on how firms access capital in a developing (or as he would have us understand, a consolidated type of capitalism) region, Schneider interprets the low skill trap as an endemic feature of developing countries, but fails to link this feature with the social and political nature of the countries in Latin America. Incorporating an identity-based perspective to understand how firms and actors access capital allows us to understand the multiple ways business actors consider societal and political dynamics in their engagement with West African firms. The practice of deregulation within ECOWAS member states represents an internal political dynamic, which results in a regionalized, institutional approach to fiscal governance. In addition, an identity-based approach centers the role of international and regional institution building in pressuring states, businesses, and multinational corporations in trying to break the low skill trap. Highlighting the process in which regional organizations and firms interact provides a political space for consensus building and for solutions to the low skill trap problem. This dynamic is present in West Africa.

Afri-Capitalism: An Identity-based Approach to Capital

Afri-capitalism is defined as the business sector discourses, practices, and innovations that allow African business actors to reconcile their culture with Western capitalism (Edozie 2017, 5). Afri-capitalism captures the essence and spirit of Pan-Africanism as a culturally driven response to global political economy that infuses African identities, aspirations, and interests into global development discourses. The framework of Afri-capitalism is a useful alternative for explicitly explaining theoretically and practically the preferences and interests of business actors in West Africa. Rather than focusing or embracing Africa's peripheral role in political economy, Afri-capitalism offers an agentic framework in which analysts do not take for granted the historic roles Africans have in shaping global economic norms and practices. (Falola and Achberger 2013; Hanson, Kararach, and Shaw 2012; Edozie 2017). As such, we can understand the development of region-centered, identity-based fiscal policy in West Africa as a reaffirmation and embrace of Pan-Africanism as a practice. The framework of Afri-capitalism also increases the visibility and scope of business sector actors and characterizes their motivations as not purely self-interested and rational, but rooted in collectiveness and partnership.

Financial Deregulation in ECOWAS Member States

Financial deregulation as a policy strategy and the spread of West African–created non-state business actors highlight the ways in which firms have opted to use and take advantage of an institutional environment that does not resemble the fiscal landscape of other regions, which resemble varying degrees of formal hierarchies and internal sanctioning/compliance measures. Thus, we see policy convergence and adaption instead of a weakening of institutions, as some VoC approaches suggest in the presence of compliance measures (Natrass 2014, 58). Financial deregulation in theory is meant to destabilize the region and produce coordination problems and decreased governing capacity in West Africa. The practice of financial deregulation in ECOWAS member states has proved to have the opposite effect. Fiscal deregulation removed hierarchy from the fiscal sector in West Africa, and overtime, deregulation has led to more competition in the financial system between transnational commercial banks, led to openness throughout the region, and increased the presence of internationalization in West Africa. This is important, as many of ECOWAS' economic sectors are fragmented and lack competition. However, a key to understanding why deregulation and financialization are important to the everyday lives of West Africans is found in the context of the labor market as the labor market is where businesses make their investment decisions and develop an understanding of the contexts in which ECOWAS and non-state business actors deem it necessary to increase financialization given the conditions of the labor market.

Labor Market Conditions in West Africa

The labor market in West Africa is characterized by low rates of urbanization and underdevelopment, as most cities represent a small percentage of their country's population. For example, in Niger, 6% of the population resides in the capital of Niamey, 7% in Ouagadougou, Burkina Faso, and 22% in Dakar, Senegal. The median age for the work force in West African cities is 18 years old. According to Roubaud and Torelli (2013), only 41% of the potential working population do not have or are not looking for a job. Students and homemakers are the largest inactive people and account for 20% of the West African workforce. Less than 4% of West Africans retire, as there is a need to continue working after 60 years old and the supply of pensions is insufficient. According to the International Labor Organization (ILO) in 2019, the average unemployment rate in West Africa is 6.64%.[6]

The rationale as to why there are disparities in the labor market in West Africa stems from the workforce's expectations. According to Afrobarometer data, most youth in West Africa believe that they are too young to work (even if they are of age), they believe that they are too educated or that they do not have the sufficient amount of education, and job seekers believe that they should be making the equivalent of 182 USD per week, which is twice the actual average earnings of an employed worker.

There is also the real and perceived problem of underemployment in West Africa. According to the data from the ILO, in ECOWAS, 26% of the work force wants to work in the public sector and 48% want to work in the informal sector. 81% of jobs in West Africa are in the informal sector (ILO 2016). For example, in 2018, 3.8% of jobs in Senegal were in the formal sector (African Development Bank 2018). The informality of the labor market in West Africa underscores the need for macroeconomic stability and structural reforms in the formal sector. The informality of the labor market does not provide security coverage, and workers in the region are forced to work in poor conditions. Taken together, job seekers often attempt to gather capital to make their own informal business, blurring the line of what is considered work and nonwork. These dynamics also show how there are little to no mechanisms available to coordinate on wage bargaining.

The West African labor market brings to bear the fact that there is a lack of institutional complementarity within the region. Some view the idea that once a specific coordination mode has emerged in one area, it pushes for complementary institutions in other spheres (Bohle and Greskovits 2009, 360) as a negative condition for doing business in the region. However, the absence of complementary institutions underscores the notion that there is policy and institutional space that firms can use to determine what kinds of actors are best suited for the region, filled by ECOWAS and its nodes of non-state business actor networks. This is not to say that system coordination is not possible or does not exist in the West African context; rather, it is to say that there may be other political, social, and economic processes at play that give way to system coordination in a different form.

When accounting for the process of regional convergence in finance, a focus on coordination through national-level analysis makes it difficult to discern the driving logics and forces of the system. Despite all of the hurdles and shortcomings of the West African labor market, it begs to question the rise of financialization in West Africa. ECOWAS and its stakeholders and business actors see the flawed labor market as an opportunity for making West Africa attractive for businesses.

ECOWAS Evolution and Convergence in Finance

As the main impetus for the creation of ECOWAS was to move the region toward more economic openness and integration, many of the early institutional policies and arrangements would deal explicitly with market liberalization. As one ECOWAS practitioner mentioned, ECOWAS's initial mandate on macroeconomic convergence was to determine the maximum level of indicators that had to do with fiscal discipline and financial stability.[7] However, prior to the creation of ECOWAS, West African countries did not view integration as a viable basis for growth and industrialization, particularly given the varied postindependence context for most member states.

Before the creation of ECOWAS, there were several attempts at regional economic integration in West Africa. Some examples include the 1958 Ghana–Guinea Union, the Ghana–Guinea–Mali Union of 1961, and the "Friendship Convention" between Ghana, Guinea, and Liberia; Ghana–Guinea–Mali and Algeria, Morocco, and Libya also formed the "Casablanca Group" common market, which dissolved after the creation of the Organization of African Unity (OAU). Another relevant attempt at a common market was between Guinea, Mali, Mauritania, and Senegal, called the Organization of the Senegal River States (OERS)—created in 1968 to develop the Senegal River basin and move toward self-reliance in agricultural development. The group dissolved after three years, in 1971.[8] Underlying these integration efforts, were narratives of self-determination, collectiveness, and kinship, core ideological features of Pan-Africanism. Despite these appeals to integration through Pan-Africanism, Nigeria was one of the few countries that opposed a political union of West African states due to the belief that the region should solidify an economic arrangement that leads to a common market. Nigeria held the idea that states, after independence, have a shared conception of how and why they need each other (Asante 1985). Ghana and countries with French colonial legacy opposed Nigeria's position, such as Cote d'Ivorie and Niger. There were also tensions between Nigeria and the European Economic Community around economic trade and liberalization. One of the points of contention was around the question of Nigeria's viability as a viable, stable, market anchor for other West African states and its ability to remain stable enough to be a reliable trading partner with the Commonwealth. Contestation over the economic liberalization of West Africa's markets eventually contributed to the region's inability to establish a pre-1970 economic community. The Biafra War also compounded the challenges to regional integration in 1966–1967.

Between Nigeria and Ghana, there was persistent posturing the two regarding what was better for West Africa. Nkrumah left the West African Currency Board and West African Airways because it could not associate with dependencies in common institutions (Ojo and Song 1979). Nkrumah cited Nigeria frequently in its reluctance to economic integration, as it feared Nigerian dominance and Nigerian relations with Britain and the Commonwealth (Wayas 1979).

Despite these early regional rivalries, the creation of ECOWAS in May 1975 signified the culmination of over 15 years of arguing and negotiating how to incorporate elements of Pan-African ideals with the need and desire to open and liberalize West African economies. While economic integration was the main driver of the creation of ECOWAS, it quickly became apparent that political instability, extra-African influence, and the potential of large-state dominance in the region would slow economic integration progress. The Pan-African ideals that justified an economic union shifted toward the region's inescapable political and security demands.

At its founding, ECOWAS' commitment to macroeconomic stability could be described as elusive at best. ECOWAS as an organization sought to maintain the centrality of the state through the delegation of institutional power. At its founding, members of the Authority Heads of State would cite the maintenance of member state sovereignty as a primary challenge to the efficacy and legitimacy of ECOWAS. In this case, one can question the extent to which some countries had a higher degree of autonomy than others could and how central ECOWAS would become to the individual fiscal policies of member states.

We begin to see a shift in ECOWAS' policy beginning in 1989 and throughout the Liberian Civil War. While this may seem unrelated to ECOWAS' regionalization efforts, we consider the Liberian Civil War to be a turning point in ECOWAS because it was the first time the ECOWAS as an area engaged in something other than economics. From 1989, ECOWAS had a number of political and economic reforms, such as the Protocol for Political Principles in 1991, the Revised Treaty of 1993, and the Protocol Relating to the Mechanism for Conflict Prevention in 1999. These institutional changes and the driving forces behind them indicated that ECOWAS would engage in regionalization, resulting in policies that were much more than fiscal and macroeconomic policies. ECOWAS was interested in transforming the organization into an entity with an identity and a penchant for collectively constructing a notion of West Africa that benefited the well-being of the people. During the 1980s, ECOWAS member states started to experiment with financial deregulation, but it was not until the Revised Treaty in 1993 that there was a push from ECOWAS for member states to start adopting harmonization policies (Ribot 2002, 19). By calling for states to develop integrative and conducive policies to the mission of ECOWAS, such as deregulation, member states would relinquish control of economic policy to the local level, all in the name of regional state-building.

Despite the overt shift to political and security-oriented regional governance, a frequent refrain and belief of ECOWAS practitioners is that fiscal and economic convergence is the most important factor in facilitating and accelerating the integration process in West Africa. Member states are frequently called on by their counterparts to "make sacrifices" needed to honor commitments to the Community. A key institutional moment for ECOWAS to begin a refocus on regional financial governance was during the forty-fifth ordinary session of the ECOWAS Council of Ministers in December 1999. The meeting included representatives from each member state and, in particular, members from the West African Monetary Agency, Committee of Governors of Central Banks, the OAU, African Economic Community (AEC), the United Nations Economic Commission for Africa (ECA), and the Coordination of the Regional Indicative Programme (RIP), among others.

The Togolese Minister for Economic Affairs, Finance, and Privatisation, Abdoul-Hamid Tidjani-Dourodjaye, in his capacity as Council Chairman, specified ECOWAS' need to shift back to "fundamental issues such as the convergence of sectoral macroeconomic policies" and "effectively applying the trade liberalization scheme."[9] According to Tidjani-Dourojaye, this refocus would be part of an organizational "facelift" which would require "sacrifices" member states. As such, deregulation and contributions to the community levy were two of the primary directives to member states to refocus on regional macroeconomic stability.

The first phase of financial sector deregulation in ECOWAS member states saw the withdrawal of monetary authorities within member states from interfering in the determination of lending rates of interest, giving commercial banks the freedom to set rates based on market conditions of supply and demand for credit (Jalloh 2014; Soyibo 1997). Many of the ECOWAS member states in the late 1980s removed credit ceilings and interest rate ceilings, and liberalized entries of financial institutions. The move toward financial sector reform was motivated by two ideas. First, ECOWAS countries stressed the need to improve their monetary control systems. This was a focal point of an ECOWAS Extraordinary Summit meeting in Lomé in May 1985, where finance ministers argued that monetary instruments in West Africa were inadequate replacing existing systems of direct control with indirect control (Journal of ECOWAS 1985, 212). Second, ECOWAS wanted financial sector reform to improve the mobilization and allocation of domestic savings and an improvement on the banking system and structure of rates in the region. Senegal, in the late 1980s, pushed a policy to reduce interest rates subsides and reduced bad debt. The Gambia and Sierra Leone liberalized interest rates and introduced prime rates to the country, while Nigeria pursued a holistic financial sector overhaul centered on diversifying its financial system (Villanueva 1998; El-Nil 1990).

The Abuja Treaty of 1991 of ECOWAS (not to be confused with the treaty by the same name creating the African Economic Community) aimed to create an inclusive West African market through trade liberalization and a single economic community. It established six stages to achieve this process, which include conceptions of ambiguous tariff stabilization and the creation of a West African monetary union and the call for member state governments to alter their domestic operations and engage in the privatization of publicly owned banks and to make the process of granting licenses to private individuals to register financial institutions easier (Jalloh 2011, 3).

In ECOWAS' formative years, member states had fluctuating economies that were susceptible to uncertainty and heavily dependent on the stability of the Nigerian oil sector. Foreign Direct Investment in ECOWAS economies mostly came from bilateral agreements. The Abuja Treaty and the Revised ECOWAS treaty created the space for ECOWAS to develop mechanisms that would make West Africa more attractive to foreign direct investment. As such, ECOWAS, under Article 53 of the Revised Treaty, created a Capital Issues committee that would focus on ensuring "the unimpeded flow of capital within the community" through removing controls on the transfer of capital, encouraging regional stock exchanges, and interlocking capital markets and stock exchanges. The Capital Issues Committee creates institutions within ECOWAS that would facilitate the ease of business in West Africa, promote diversification in West African markets, and improve trade information networks to induce transparency. Additionally, the creation of the West African Monetary Association (WAMA) created in 1996 and the transformation of the ECOWAS Fund to the ECOWAS Investment and Development Bank in 1999 all serve as significant, early institutional moves to orient regional fiscal policy toward convergence.

As the ECOWAS Executive Committee is considering how to stabilize the macroeconomic environment in West Africa, it also began to consider the viability of a common West African currency. Charles Konan Banny, head of the Committee of Governors of Central Banks and Governor of the Central Bank of West African States (BCEAO), argued that the financial organs of ECOWAS, the Capital Issues committee and WAMA, could help facilitate a move toward a single currency in the region, which would be a key to moving ECOWAS toward a bank-centric region and a place where private banking and business could enjoy success.[10] His argument was informed by recent progress by West African Central Banks in coordinating the creation of ECOWAS Travelers' Checks and the establishment of the Credit Guarantee Fund, with WAMA directed to monitor the facilitation of ECOWAS traveler check implementation. The key component to the financialization process here would be the eventual transfer of the facilitation of the traveler check regime to the private sector "within the shortest possible time." The creation of a single monetary zone and the relegation of financial management to the private sector helped create the institutional space and conditions for financialization in the region. As such, following an extraordinary summit meeting in January 2001, ECOWAS officials finally made due on their promise to set plans in motion to create a Single Currency for West Africa called the Eco.

Initially, the Eco would first be extended to former French colonial West African states (who are on the Communatué financière d'Afrique/African Financial Community (CFA) Franc), hoping that Anglophone states would adopt the currency by 2020. ECOWAS created the West African Monetary Institute (WAMI), which would be responsible for overseeing the feasibility of developing the Eco. WAMI's goal is to minimize the effects of asymmetric economic shocks by developing convergence criteria and, over time, facilitating real trade integration, financial sector integration, and systemic regional harmonization. WAMI consists of ECOWAS' Authority Heads of State, a convergence council, a technical committee, a central bank, a research institute, Secretariat, stabilization and cooperation fund, and a supervisory authority.

WAMI focuses on ten criteria for convergence—four primary criteria and six secondary criteria, in order to ensure that the Eco can be created without significant repercussion. These convergence criteria undergird the five strategic pillars of instituting the Eco and regional integration more broadly.

WAMI has made it a point to highlight that there are significant cultural and economic differences between the countries that are prospectively joining the Eco, highlighting the differences in governing structures (contrasting Nigeria's federalist system versus Ghana's unitary system) as hurdles to integration and potential limitations to convergence. Although WAMI's strategic plan highlights the areas where convergence is and is not possible, the Eco has failed to launch.

Beyond the technical difficulties in establishing the Eco as a single West African currency, the Eco has been a point of political contention in

ECOWAS. In a summit meeting in early 2019, the Authority Heads of State committed to reigniting efforts to establishing the Eco by 2020. However, in December of 2019, members of the West African Economic and Monetary Union (WAEMU), a group consisting of seven former French colonies and Guinea Bissau who use the West African CFA Franc as their common currency, agreed to significant reforms to the West African CFA Franc, with the most drastic of those reforms being the renaming of the West African CFA Franc to the "Eco." In an announcement by President Alassane Outtara of Cote d'Ivoire and French President Emmanuel Macron, the new "Eco" will see a reduced role in oversight by the French government, the removal of a French representative on the BCEAO, and WAEMU countries are no longer required to keep half of their exchange reserves in Paris. However, the West African CFA Franc is still pegged to the Euro.

This move by WAMEU reignited political tensions within ECOWAS. Nigeria, for instance, has accused France and Cote d'Ivoire of "hijacking" the single currency process by adopting the name "Eco" and excluding the non-WAMEU states from the process. Officials from Cote d'Ivoire accuse Nigeria of being hypocrites as Nigeria has closed its borders to Benin and Niger violating ECOWAS' trade liberalization scheme. However, these arguments should not be considered purely on colonial-linguistic lines, as Ghana has pleaded with WAEMU states to include nonmembers into the currency scheme and has condemned Nigeria's border closings.

Taken together, the efforts of WAMI and the political contention of a single currency are important for a couple of reasons. One reason is that a common currency agenda runs counter to the capital market environment that ECOWAS set out to create. Put simply, a disconnect exists between money markets and capital markets. The tension lies in making West Africa "bank-centric," enabling short-term investment and fundraising, lending to the pathologies mentioned in the complexion of the labor market sector. However, by virtue of ECOWAS' desire to increase foreign direct investment (FDI), it also believes in capital market principles in that capital markets mobilize long-term debt and equity finance for investment in long-term assets (Allen, Otchere, and Senbet 2011). Another reason is that the creation of a common currency in practice contradicts WAMA's initial call for domestic financial systems to deregulate, which member states abided by. The creation of a West African Capital Markets Integration Council in 2013 and the Bourse Régionale des Valeurs Mobiliéres (BVRM) in 1998 are evidence that ECOWAS countries are striving to improve capital flows such as FDI by regionalizing the stock exchange. Another key institutional development in ECOWAS has been the creation of a private sector department in 2007, charged with developing strategies developing strategies to mobilize the private sector to promote greater ease of business (Iheduru 2012, 221).

The expansion of the financial institutions in ECOWAS, coupled with ECOWAS' focus on financial sector reform, demonstrates ECOWAS' attempts at regional convergence in finance. While the struggle for convergence in currency tell one end of the story, deregulation as a practice tells another part of how West Africa as a region has created a space for finance to dwell.

Deregulation as a Practice

A characteristic of ECOWAS member states is that they have large, active rural settings (Schrader 2001; Bauer and Taylor 2005). As a result, rural elites often find themselves trying to leverage their political positions against national elites. Boone (2003, 361) argues that local level elites (chiefs, farmers, merchants, etc.) occupy different positions in social relations and that they present variations on their interests that present challenges to national governments—particularly when it comes to institutional strategies that national governments devise when it comes to governing and taxing the country side. National governments also recognize and legitimate these local rural elites, often giving deference to the communal structures and traditional legacies of local, precolonial political structures. Rural leaders in this regard are political actors that national governments must engage. In this vein, a deconcentrated state apparatus can provide political infrastructure for power sharing with local elites, usurpation, or deference to the rural structure. Boone (2003, 365) argues the first two points in discussing the strategies rural elites use to leverage their political power.

After colonization, local governments were used as administration units, used to supply health care, education, infrastructure, and taxation (Therkildsen 2001, 82). Deregulation in practice ended up being an extension of central administration. Senegal maintained a system of ruling party control and administrative oversight after independence in 1976, which put a stranglehold on local autonomy (Nigeria and Ghana in the 1970s and 1980s also gave special functions and protection to local governments, but in practice, none of these governments had meaningful policy-making powers (UNCDF 2000, 2).

However, by 1994, there is a shift in how ECOWAS countries engaged in deregulation as a practice. At the ECOWAS-sponsored Burkina Faso conference on decentralization in West Africa in 1994, member states argued various positions on deregulation:

- Ivory Coast considers [deregluation] to be a "pragmatic process leading to the sharing of power between central and local levels";
- For Mauritania, [deregulation] is "an institutional landmark, a tool for democratization and a way of promoting local development";
- For Senegal, [deregulation] is "a fundamental element of a learning process in democracy and people's participation in development";
- For Guinea, "deregulation is a project for society based on natural solidarity, oriented towards development";
- Mali sees deregulation as "the best available instrument to use in reorganizing the State";

- For the Cape Verde Islands, [deregulation] is "a tool used in achieving national solidarity";
- For Benin, "deregulation is an instrument to be used in promoting grassroots democracy and local development";
- Burkina Faso expects that "deregulation should reinforce local democracy, Grassroots democracy and local development" (Mbassi 1995, 24).

Member states began to argue that deregulation would also bring macroeconomic stability and public sector equity (Mamdani 1996). ECOWAS believed that deregulation would result in a situation where central governments would also redistribute the region (Conyers 2000, 8). There were also thoughts within ECOWAS that deregulation would be able to serve as a bargaining chip and bring secessionists and other subnational groups to the political table. For instance, during the concurrent civil conflicts in Liberia and Sierra Leone, particularly in the ECOWAS peace plan, the Yamoussoukro Accord (1993) Part II Sections A and B, deregulation was used as a strategy to get the Liberian government and Charles Taylor to agree to a transitional government. The view of the ECOWAS Monitoring Group (ECOMOG) throughout the conflict mediation process was that agreeing to the accords and utilizing deregulation as a way to get all parties equally involved in the transition government in Liberia would aid in state legitimation.

ECOWAS member states provided revenue to local authorities by giving them portions of national tax revenues, empowering local governments to collect land for themselves, and collecting income and commodity taxes locally. The logic behind this form of deregulation was to prop up the private sector to accommodate the rise and proliferation of indigenous cross-border regional banking and financial services. Deregulation as an all-encompassing political strategy in West Africa contextualizes the importance of high-level activity in the banking and financial sector, as investors and private sector actors in West Africa could all see that they could not rely on bilateral or domestic banking and financial services to provide the access to capital needed to run and/or create business.

Financialization in West Africa

Regionalization processes from ECOWAS as an organization and deregulation policies from ECOWAS member states provided the space for us to contextualize how the nature of business, banking, finance, and capitalism have changed throughout the years. In the previous decade, 30 of the top 200 banks in Africa are in ECOWAS and the combined assets of the top 15 West African banks ($86.9 billion) exceeded the $70.2 billion combined GDP (gross domestic product) of nine ECOWAS member states; $86.9 billion is also about 45% of Nigeria's GDP (Iheduru 2012, 278–280). West African-based financial firms and banks were central in keeping up with the annual 4–5% growth during the 2008 financial crisis. Investors in an Attractiveness of

Africa survey by Ernst and Young in 2011 found that the changing character of West African finance comes from the growth in intra-African investment into new FDI projects, growing at an annual pace of 21% between 2003 and 2011. By contrast, emerging economies outside of Africa grew their FDI at an annual pace of 9% (Otty and Ajen 2011, 31).

The rise in commercial banking has had implications on the banking clientele in West Africa. For instance, Cote d'Ivoire, Senegal, and Gambia have had increased competition from microfinance firms and new business strategies from foreign investors, leading to diversification in traditional industries such as trade and hospitalities (IMF Country Report 2012). Cross-regional banking has expanded because private equity groups have been purchasing domestic banks in an effort to expand their markets. Nigerian-based companies such as Stanbic-IBTC and Ecobank as well as Moroccan financial groups purchase banks within West Africa to expand their markets. A report on the financial depth of ECOWAS in 2013 states that the groups (incorporated as subsidies) who purchase domestic banks are funded through local deposits. The domestic orientation of the purchased banks provides a mutual benefit for the company and the local banking structure, which explains why the direct impact of the global crisis was mild in West Africa. Stress tests on banking systems in ECOWAS also indicate there are limited interest rate and liquidity risks within the banks of West Africa because of cross-border banking. The stress tests included potential and actual economic shocks, sectoral risks like defaults on loans, and liquidity shocks.

Financialization manifests itself in a couple of ways in ECOWAS. First, functions typically left for central banks in member states to handle are now outsourced to regional institutions. The ECOWAS-created Ecobank Transnational Incorporation has led this effort. Created by the West African Chamber of Commerce and ECOWAS as a regional investment bank, Ecobank started with $100 million authorized shared capital and paid $32 million in capital to individuals and other banking institutions within the region when global banking institutions pulled out of West Africa. Ecobank is the sixth largest banking institution in Africa and is the first African banking institution to expand throughout the continent and has branches outside of the continent. It now manages over $10 billion worth of assets and capital. Ecobank has also taken an interest in building its capacity in service provision in the labor market. An official of the Ecobank Foundation mentioned an institutional focus on creating high-quality jobs, creating avenues for increased technical skills for young people, and eliminating boundaries for entry-level employment.[11] The official points specifically to ECOWAS and Ecobank's coordination in providing capacity-building workshops on entrepreneurship and enterprise development, skills acquisition, and training to mobilize the labor market. With a youth-driven, mobilized labor market, West Africa becomes a place where businesses can be comfortable with their investments.[12]

ECOWAS has also taken the limits of the labor market and has advocated for the facilitation on the ease of business through financialization by creating networks such as the BIAWE. ECOWAS BIAWE's goal is to strengthen and engage the capacity of rural women and provide support services to women entrepreneurs. ECOWAS BIAWE serves as an avenue for women in business to share knowledge on conformity in business standards and to create employment through small business development and acceleration of growth (ECOWAS 2015). Stanbic-IBTC has worked closely with ECOWAS BIAWE to provide capital and resources to West African women–led startups. In contrast, private equity firm African Capital Alliance invested in businesses created through ECOWAS BIAWE.[13] The labor market in West Africa, typically conceived as a hurdle to the ease of business, is reappropriated by regional actors to develop business networks to mobilize the West African workforce and provide avenues that circumvent central governments their control of the workforce. Business actors such as Ecobank firmly believe that as people have more access and accumulate jobs, there will be more use for their commercial banking services. Representatives from Ecobank and African Capital Alliance point to the transitory nature of West Africa and believe that the future of business and finance in West Africa is not tied to the successes and failures of undiversified country economies, citing that West Africans want "mobile" and "dynamic" businesses that span the region. The coordination of strategies by ECOWAS and business actors to combat the realities of the labor market provides some context as to how financialization becomes a strategy and method of regional convergence.

Second, private firms have been given the authority to make up for the lack of common currency in the region by providing payment systems for formal and informal trade, providing remittances for migrant workers, and enabling foreign exchange transactions (Iheduru 2012, 225). Ecobank, for example, has created an ATM system that allows one to travel with one form of payment throughout West Africa, a region with eight different currencies, without consequence. As a result, access to finance has increased substantially in ECOWAS countries.

Regional Convergence Through ECOWAS BIAWE

The practice of deregulation and financialization created a space for the business and financial institutions of ECOWAS to collaborate and engage the region through investment on the local level. In June 2012, ECOWAS and New Partnership for Africa's Development (NEPAD) signed an agreement to create the ECOWAS BIAWE. Though the initiative was funded by the NEPAD Spain Fund, ECOWAS practitioners in the Macrofinance Directorate of the Finance Commission were instrumental in fostering this agreement.

The purpose of creating ECOWAS BIAWE was to develop rural business entrepreneurs across the region. Francois Ouedraogo, the project manager for ECOWAS BIAWE, stressed that the creation of the incubator would ensure capacity building through technical and financial support to enable women to pursue their maximum potential and the main method of this support would come from the support of regional partners and private investment stakeholders. Ouedraogo describes the process of negotiating the creation of ECOWAS BIAWE:

> We were in a meeting on the status of business investment the region, took place in Lomé. We had two very persuasive representatives invited from the ECOWAS Business Forum, a woman from Sierra Leone and another from Burkina. They stressed how important it was to build the capacity of women in their countries, particularly in the agriculture sector. They said the women in their countries had great ideas and they needed the financial backing of regional business to make the ideas into reality. The women were backed by MacDonald S. Goanue, [Director of Research and strategic planning] who also emphasized that in his native Liberia, a project focused on the improvement of lives would be most welcome. So it was from here that we put a proposal together to work with NEPAD. But it was my job to find other private actors to engage in the building of this initiative.[14]

During the drafting process of the Memorandum of Understanding (MoU) between ECOWAS and NEPAD, Allieu Sesay, the Finance Commissioner for ECOWAS, and a Sierra Leonean himself, pushed for the feasibility study of the program to start in Sierra Leone and Burkina, stressing a crisis of the overall economies in these countries and the profound neglect of women and children in the said countries. Sesay's motivation for improving the quality of the business environment for rural women stemmed from his previous positions as consultant economist for the African Development Bank, the World Bank, and the European Union. Among his staff, he is considered to be the expert on how to incorporate business into sectoral policy. During the initial meetings during the drafting of the ECOWAS/NEPAD MoU, Sesay advocated strongly to incorporate EBID and the ECOWAS Business Forum to create and develop a reliable structure for women to develop as business people.

In doing so, ECOWAS practitioners working for Sesay were aware that the institutional environment was not conducive to creating a sustainable program with ECOWAS' funding woes. As one practitioner mentions:

> Despite the excitement by Mr. Sesay, we very much thought the feasibility of this incubator was not possible. We have member states who still decide not to contribute to the community levy and we are strapped with budget issues, but Mr. Sesay and other believed we could get the external funding to help facilitate the initial study, so we went ahead.[15]

This indicated that one of the strategies for building this program was to rely on external funding to support ECOWAS' activism, through the use of the

MoU. This highlights the importance of an MoU to the convergence process, in that MoUs do not serve as merely documents that create an agreement between two parties, but the process of drafting an MoU has strategic implication, particularly for ECOWAS. In the case of BIAWE, there were two strategic plans in place. The first, mentioned above, was to create a narrative stressing the importance of external funding to creating the program. The second strategy was to use BIAWE to build stronger partnerships with regional financial stakeholders and to use the financial institutions of ECOWAS to take advantage of business investors in West Africa who stressed a region-centric investment policy.

After the drafting of the MoU between ECOWAS and NEPAD, the first feasibility study for BIAWE launched in July 2014 in Sierra Leone and Burkina Faso. The feasibility study focused on the agriculture sector and looked at land disparities between men and women. For example, in Sierra Leone, women cannot own land and can participate formally in small-scale farming and agricultural activities only if they are authorized to work by their husbands. As a result, the implementation phase of BIAWE included provisions to give access to financing for rural women to participate in both the formal and informal agricultural sectors. Investment in BIAWE would also include improving value sharing mechanisms to provide women a level playing field once their businesses become self-sustaining. Ouedraogo stressed the importance of informal business investment by West African firms because of the importance ECOWAS also placed on social development. BIAWE, in this regard, is an initiative that is focused not only on the betterment of African Women throughout the region, but also as a way for the interactions between small-scale informal business networks to form and socialize local level businesses into a member state's formal economy.

The role of ECOWAS practitioners in creating ECOWAS BIAWE initially was to provide and deploy a strategy to get the incubator created and funded. As it moves toward implementation across West Africa beyond Sierra Leone and Burkina Faso, ECOWAS practitioners in the ECOWAS Business Forum and EBID are working to create networks between BIAWE and other regional finance networks. These networks include the West African Trade and Investment Hub, West African Capital Markets Integration Council, and the Aspen Network of Development Entrepreneurs in West Africa. Hyacenth Okwu, the Vice President in the Finance Directorate of the ECOWAS Commission, stated that building these networks is a necessity and an active strategy by the practitioners in the finance commission to create a linkage and investment pipeline for business people in the region. Okwu also stressed the importance of training of finance facilitators to help businesses curated in BIAWE develop business plans and facilitate loan applications.[16]

ECOWAS BIAWE and its constitutive networks are examples of regional convergence on improving the West African business environment. The activities of ECOWAS member states, particularly allowing commercial banks and private investment to play the role it does in the business environment, indicate that ECOWAS practitioners have motivations to improve the "ways of doing business" and are also interested in a more inclusive business environment. Through deregulation, financialization emerged and also a collective desire by ECOWAS practitioners in finance to utilize new and potential sources for access to capital to build an initiative that would affect the people of the region on a local level and embed practices of business that are uniquely West African. Despite the efforts, ECOWAS still struggles with road harassment and poor infrastructure in its member states, making cross-border business initiatives difficult.

In looking at ECOWAS BIAWE, the drivers of convergence were the ECOWAS practitioners attempting to shape the nature of interactions, while soliciting external help to overcome institutional shortcomings. BIAWE is still in the implementation phase; however, as ECOWAS practitioners continue to pursue their interests in the initiative, one would expect to see a form of institutionalization occur and BIAWE would be integrated into the ECOWAS Business and Finance infrastructures.

Conclusion

While it is evident that there is a pattern of the regionalization of finance and banking in West Africa, what does it say about financialization as a policy? For instance, if we look at financialization in the vein of Krippner (2005; 2011), the narrative presented gauges the behavior of financial firms and the growth of the financial sector, with no implications on the growth of profits in the financial sector. This chapter examined how the organization of economic activity in ECOWAS has implications on collectivity and regional cooperation. However, examining how regionalization and deregulation as political processes and strategies lead to financialization has broader implications for the study of regional fiscal governance in the developing world.

By highlighting the process in which ECOWAS moves toward the practice of financialization, it provides a context where we can examine empirically the substance of accumulation, the implications of financialization on economic growth, and how profit is generated in the region. Krippner (2005, 190) poses the question: "should the practice of contracting out-financial functions once executed [in-house] count as evidence of financialization?" and answers the question by suggesting that although outsourcing tasks is not a new phenomenon, its sectoral location vis-à-vis shifting firm boundaries—and the prevalence of changing ownership structures (in ECOWAS' case from the local/domestic/national to the regional)—is what is important to financialization. As such, where this particular study can build on Krippner's questions is to employ a longitudinal time series analysis to measure how outsourcing over time affects income, capital accumulation, and development indicators such as GDP growth.

Financialization in ECOWAS also highlights how there is an emerging form of regional governance through private authority. This private authority is interested in protecting investors so that investors may raise capital. A result is the emergence of policy entrepreneurs that advocate for laws and policies within ECOWAS to protect minority shareholders and policies that make it easy for them to become controlling shareholders (World Bank 2013, 51). The dynamic of policy entrepreneurs also working in conjunction with firms, regional banks, and MNCs has implications on which the important actors are in an examination of the VoC. This particular combination of actors leads one to hypothesize if the role of policy entrepreneurs in ECOWAS might serve as a complementarity of financialization. Future implications for this research applied more toward testing the compatibility of VoC in West Africa might view regional convergence and deregulation as complementarities, which would also elicit a broader examination of regionalization and deregulation in other developing areas within and outside of Africa.

Notes

1 According to the European Systemic Risk Board, sovereign risks arise when a government has higher expenditures than tax revenues, resulting in irreversible amounts of debt that make it difficult for countries to comply with its contractual debt obligations and expose the country's financial sector to market risks such as interest rate risk, inflation risk, and exchange rate risks.

2 Ba (2016, 12) highlights the implications of institutionalization understood not in terms of strictly enforced, rule-bound structures, but in terms of an expansive view of institutionalization that focuses on the normative and social dimensions of institutionalization, in the context of South East Asia. Ba's example of institutionalization offers a useful parallel to the effects of social practices on deeper organizational institutionalization in West Africa.

3 This information came from an interview with the head of Public Sector affairs with Stanbic IBTC, Adekunle Fatokun, June 2, 2016.

4 See Ayyagary et al. (2014) on the role of labor markets on regional convergence in developing countries.

5 For more on the "firm's eye view" perspective, see Hall and Soskice 2001, Chapter 1.

6 Total unemployment (% of total labor force)—ECOWAS member states. https://data.worldbank.org/indicator/SL.UEM.TOTL.ZS?locations=ZG (date retrieved February 10, 2020).

7 Interview, ECOWAS Macroeconomic Commission member, Abuja, Nigeria, June 2016.

8 For more information on these organizations, see Aguibou Yansane (1977). "The State of Economic Integration in North West African South of the Sahara: The Emergence of the Economic Community of West African States." *African Studies Review* 20(2): 63–87.

9 ECOWAS Forty-Fifth Session of the Council of Ministers (Final Report), Lome, Togo December 5–7, 1999 ECW/CM. XLV/12/Rev.1.

10 Committee of Central Bank Governors speech, December 1999.

11 Interview, Ecobank Official, Lomé, Togo, June 2016.

12 Ibid.

13 Author interview with Adekunle Fatokun, June 2016.

14 Francois Ouedraogo, Interview EBID, Lomé, Togo, October 25, 2016.
15 Anonymous Interview, ECOWAS Finance, Abuja, Nigeria, October 2016.
16 Interview, Hyacenth Okwu, ECOWAS Commission, October 21, 2016.

References

African Development Bank. 2018. “West Africa Economic Outlook.”

Allen, Franklin, Isaac, Otchere, and Lemma W. Senbet. 2011. “African Financial Systems: A Review.” Review of Development Finance 1(2): 79–113.

Asante, Samuel KB. 1985. “ECOWAS/CEAO: Conflict and Cooperation in West Africa.” In The Future of Regionalism in Africa. London: Macmillan, 74–95.

Babarinde, Olufemi. 2012. “The Private Equity Market in Africa: Trends, Opportunities, Challenges, and Impact.” Journal of Private Equity 16(1): 56–73. DOI: 10.3905/jpe.2012.16.1.056

Bauer, Gretchen, and Scott D. Taylor. 2005. Politics in Southern Africa: State and Society in Transition. Boulder: Lynne Rienner Publishers.

Bohle, Dorothee, and Béla Greskovits. 2009. “Varieties of Capitalism and Capitalism «tout court».” European Journal of Sociology/Archives Européennes de Sociologie 50(3): 355–386.

Boone, Catherine. 2003. “State, Capital, and the Politics of Banking Reform in Sub-Saharan Africa.” Comparative Politics 37(4): 401–420. DOI: 10.3303/CET1756052

Conyers, D. 1999. Decentralisation: A Conceptual Analysis, Ministers’ Conference on Local Government in Eastern and Southern Africa, Victoria Falls, Zimbabwe (reproduced in MDP-ESA Newsletter 2000).

ECOWAS. 2015. Annual Report “ECOWAS at 40: Achievements, Challenges, and Prospects”.

Edozie, Rita Kiki. 2017. “Pan” Africa Rising: The Cultural Political Economy of Nigeria’s Afri-Capitalism and South Africa’s Ubuntu Business. New York, NY: Springer.

Epstein, Gerald A. 2005. “Introduction.” In Financialization and the World Economy, ed. Gerald A. Epstein. Northampton: Edward Elgar Publishing.

Falola, Toyin, and Jessica Achberger, eds. 2013. The Political Economy of Development and Underdevelopment in Africa. Vol. 10. New York: Routledge.

Hanson, Kobena, George Kararach, and T. Shaw, eds 2012. Rethinking Development Challenges for Public Policy: Insights from Contemporary Africa. New York, NY: Springer.

Hearn, Bruce Allen. 2011. “The Effects of Banking Relationship, Legal Origin, Private Equity and Lead Managers on the Performance of West African IPO Firms.” South African Journal of Economics 79(4): 430–451. DOI: 10.1111/j.1813-6982.2011.01285.x

Hix, Simon. 2013. What’s Wrong with the Europe Union and How to Fix it. Hoboken, New Jersey: John Wiley & Sons.

Iheduru, Okechukwu C. 2012. “Regional Integration and the Private Authority of Banks in West Africa1.” International Studies Review 14(2): 273–302. DOI: 10.1111/j.1468-2486.2012.01112.x

ILO. 2016. Women and Men in the Informal Economy: A Statistical Picture. International Labour Office – Geneva: ILO.

International Monetary. 2012. "The Gambia: Staff Report for the 2011 Article IV Consultation." Washington DC. https://doi.org/10.5089/9781463935108.002

Journal of ECOWAS. 1985. "Official Journal of the Economic Community of West African States." Abuja.

Krippner, Greta R. 2005. "The Financialization of the American Economy." Socio-Economic Review 3(2): 173–208.

Krippner, Greta R. 2011. Capitalizing on Crisis: The Political Origins of the Rise of Finance. Cambridge, Massachusetts: Harvard University Press.

Lewis, Peter, and Howard Stein. 1997. "Shifting Fortunes: The Political Economy of Financial Liberalization in Nigeria." World Development 25(1): 5–22. DOI: 10.1016/S0305-750X(96)00085-X

Mamdani, Mahmood. 1996. Citizen and Subject: Contemporary Africa and the Legacy of Late Colonialism. 1st ed. Princeton: Princeton University Press.

Mattli, Walter. 1999. The Logic of Regional Integration: Europe and Beyond. Cambridge: Cambridge University Press.

Mbassi, J.P. Elong (ed.). 1995. La décentralisation en Afrique de l'Ouest. Report of the conference on Decentralization in West Africa, Ouagadougou, 5-8 April. Cotonou, Benin: PDM and CEDA.

Moravcsik, Andrew. 1998. "Centralization or Fragmentation? Europe Facing the Challenges of Deepening, Diversity, and Democracy." New York: Council on Foreign Relations Press.

Nattrass, Nicoli. 2014. "A South African variety of capitalism?." New Political Economy 19(1): 56–78.

Ojo, A. T., and A. Song. 1979. "Capital Market and Industrialization in the Ecowas." Journal of Management Studies 11(2), 13–18.

Otty, Mark, and Ajen Sita. 2011. "It's Time for Africa." Ernst & Young's: Africa Attractiveness Survey. United Kingdom: Ernst & Young.

Pollack, Mark A. 1997. "Delegation, Agency, and Agenda Setting in the European Community." International Organization 51(1): 99–134.

Pollack, Mark A. 2003.The Engines of European Integration: Delegation, Agency, and Agenda Setting in the EU. Oxford: OUP.

Reinhart, Carmen M, and Ioannis Tokalidis. 2003. "Financial Liberalisation: The African Experience." Journal of African Economics 12(Suppl. 2): 53–88. DOI: 10.1093/jae/12.suppl_2.ii53

Ribot, Jesse C. 2002. African Decentralization: Local Actors, Powers and Accountability. Geneva: UNRISD.

Roubaud, Francois, and Constance Torelli. 2013. "Employment, Unemployment, and Working Conditions in Urban Labor Markets of Sub-Saharan Africa: Main Stylized Facts." In Philippe de Vreyer and Francois Roubaud (eds.), Urban Labor Markets in Sub-Saharan Africa. Washington, D.C.: World Bank, 37–80.

Schneider, Ben Ross. 2009. "Hierarchical Market Economies and Varieties of Capitalism in Latin America." Journal of Latin American Studies 41(3): 553–575.

Schneider, Sebastian. 2014. Varieties of Capitalism, Varieties of Crisis Response Bank Bailouts in Comparative Perspective. No. 21/2014. Papers on International Political Economy (PIPE).

Schraeder, Peter J. 2001. New Directions in Francophone West African Foreign Policies. London: Lynne Rienner, 41–44.

Therkildsen, Ole. 2001. "Understanding Taxation in Poor African Countries: A Critical Review of Selected Perspectives." Forum for Development Studies 28(1): 99–123.

UNCDF. 2000. "Results-Oriented Annual Report of the United Nations Capital Development Fund."

Wayas, Joseph. 1979. "Clearing Away the Illusions." In Nigeria's Leadership Role in Africa. London: Palgrave Macmillan, 20–27.

World Bank. 2013. Doing Business 2014: Understanding Regulations for Small and Medium-Size Enterprises. Washington, DC: World Bank Group. DOI: 10.1596/978-0-8213-9984-2

6 Taking Stock of Convergence and Agency in West Africa

Has West Africa become a safer region since the creation of ECOWAS?

> The decline of interstate violence and civil wars in West Africa, and the greater prominence of ECOWAS in conflict management, are perhaps indications that the security situation of West Africa didn't turn out to be as gloomy as [forecasted] two decades ago. But there are important lessons that have been learnt. The organisation should support and safeguard the rights of its citizens to stage peaceful protest as a way of balancing the excesses of politicians…
>
> ECOWAS should appoint individuals who are not former heads of state and do not hold political office as regional mediators. Given Nigeria's mammoth internal challenges and weakened political clout, other countries within the region must step up and drive the organisation to achieve its mandate of becoming a community of people rather than an institution that enhances the status and profile of subversive regimes.

In this book, I present a framework for understanding the institutional development of ECOWAS, by highlighting processes of convergence and agency that mediate the interests of the region's heads of state while also bringing together disparate actors in the region. In doing so, ECOWAS and its practitioners create and rely on particular norms and practices to manage regional governance. The book makes the argument that ECOWAS practitioners, as conduits of region-building, rely on their practical understandings of the organization and the agency they acquire through institutional autonomy to determine and shape the realm of possibility in regional governance. My framework argues that region-building is neither given nor is it inherently limited by the constraints of realpolitik in West Africa; instead, region-building is a negotiated, argumentative process that works to create linkages between ECOWAS and other regional governance stakeholders, such as NGOs, regional civil society organizations, private businesses, and development partners. These linkages aid practitioners in building acceptable, durable, and dependable modes of governance. ECOWAS practitioners rely on their ability

DOI: 10.4324/9780429436734-6

to draw from distinct institutional cultures to reinforce convergence practices and to discern who and what relationships matter to regional governance.

Despite ECOWAS's innovations and push to include more regional stakeholders into the region-building project, West African regional governance still has gaps and challenges. Mali experienced two coups over 18 months in 2020 and 2021, and the critics considered ECOWAS's response to be inconsistent. Overlapping public health crises continue to challenge and stress regional health infrastructures, such as the COVID-19 global pandemic, the Ebola Virus epidemic, and an outbreak of Marburg virus disease. These kinds of challenges are not unique to West Africa; however, this book argues that the West African region is uniquely positioned to handle these challenges.

The foundational ideas and practices of ECOWAS's founding reflect how the institution and the actors therein understand ECOWAS' reason for being. While these foundational ideas and practices might be viewed as constraints to institutional change, the processes of convergence and agency characterize what is within the realm of possibility in regional governance. Given the contested nature of ECOWAS's founding and the persistent tensions among West African states at ECOWAS's founding and beyond, one might not have expected ECOWAS to be a durable institution. The historical trajectory of ECOWAS is explained by the processes of convergence and agency laid out in this work. What drives the process of convergence and agency and ultimately the durability of ECOWAS is the extent to which its practitioners can leverage their autonomy and agency to create an inclusive form of regional governance. Practitioners can engage regional actors beyond the state and conceive of regional cooperation not as merely cooperation between states, but as cooperation between a diversity of actors, ideas, and the process in which these actors and ideas come together to produce mutual meanings and understandings of the region.

In this book, I advance the concept of practitioner-led regionalisms as integral to the region-building process. A practitioner-led regionalism emphasizes the composition of regional actors, the process in which they acquire agency, and the significance of the relationships they form with other regional actors. Rather than emphasizing the structural and material constraints of region-building, I argue that a process-driven, practitioner account of region-building provides a lens and framework to examine how ideas about region-building are diffused across governance scales and how these ideas develop a localized context. Practitioners are integral to region-building due to their capacities as policy initiators and their ability to draw from background knowledge about ECOWAS to discern what is permissible.

ECOWAS practitioners use networking and organizational dynamism to converge the region and acquire their agency. Chapter 3 provides three examples of how practitioners engage in these practices: (1) relying on path-dependent understandings of the principle of noninterference to converge institutional norms and practices toward the bolstering of democracy and good governance; (2) creating partnerships with West African Networking for

Peacebuilding (WANEP), International Red Cross, and others to clarify and embed peace and security practices into the region; and (3) highlighting the process in which practitioners use institutional mechanisms such as training and policy creation to display their agency as autonomous actors in the institution.

Similarly, Chapter 4 shows how institutional changes and updates to the original mandate of West African Health Organization (WAHO) gave practitioners the institutional space to serve as primary actors in regional health governance. Organizational dynansim in WAHO enabled WAHO practitioners to have more sway over the strategic direction of WAHO, while networking allowed practitioners to bring together regional health stakeholders to curate resources for the unit and signal the normative priorities of ECOWAS in the realm of public health. Chapter 5 highlights the increased significance of private capital proliferating across West Africa and the recognition by ECOWAS practitioners to engage in processes of financialization. The slow progress of a regional common currency, coupled with the effects of financial decentralization in ECOWAS member states, created the institutional space for practitioners to engage more directly with private economic actors. The institutional space provided civilians in member states with tools to overcome financial hurdles such as capital and business development.

Theoretical Implications

This study of region-building and regionalism in West Africa has important theoretical implications of how we study the relationship between norms and practices, the effects of institutional change, and the development of regional governance in West Africa.

This book combines practice theory, constructivism, and historical institutionalism as a means to theorize and conceptualize processes of region-building. For scholars of institutionalism, this book provides a framework that attempts to bridge the need for a theory of institutional change and a need for a theory of institutional effects (Farell 2018). Embedded in the process of convergence and agency is acknowledging path dependence, particularly the enduring role of founding arguments and original institutional design, while also acknowledging that institutions are indeed fluid. As Thelen and Mahoney (2010) suggest, the cumulative effects of incremental institutional change allow for institutions' survival and position them as significant political actors. The approach in this book takes this perspective a step further, arguing that institutional change, incremental or drastic, also creates opportunity structures for institutional actors to acquire agency.

As constructivist and comparative regionalism literature continues to grapple with the construction and process of regional identity and community building, this book does not take for granted the assumption that African agency and identity formation are merely by-products of a homogenous alignment with the tenets of Pan-Africanism, or that regionalism in Africa is merely a venue for mingling elites. Centralizing the role of practitioners as drivers of the regional project in West Africa offers a theoretical frame to contextualize how regional governance in West Africa obtains its local character. While one may conceive of practitioners as elite actors, the book argues that their autonomy allows them to include those in the regional project who can define, redefine, and reinforce political and social values in ECOWAS. The book theorizes and identifies the specific mechanisms that allow practitioners to have an influential role in region-building, which can also serve as a basis for comparison to other regional economic communities (RECs) across Africa. What makes West Africa and ECOWAS distinct from other RECs is the degree to which norms and practices are institutionalized and reinforced by practitioners to create deliberative spaces and modal responses to regional governance issues.

Recognizing the "governance turn" in comparative regionalism (Borzel and Risse 2016), the processes of convergence and agency illuminated in this book provide a basis for explaining not only how various regional stakeholders come together to shape regional governance in West Africa but also the processes and conditions that drive the actors of regional governance. Thus, combining institutional perspectives with constructivist/practice perspectives improves the ability to compare the composition of regional arrangements and explain variation in institutional design and impact of institutional change on institutional design.

Specifically, for scholars of African regionalism, this study contributes to the growing research on African international organizations and the agency of their bureaucracies (Tieku, Ganzle, and Trondal 2020; Ganzle, Trondal, and Kuhn 2019). This growing body of research on African international bureaucracies emphasizes the embeddedness of informal practices of international bureaucrats and the temporal contracting of international staff. This book juxtaposes the reliance on short-term contracted staffing with the embedded knowledge and understanding of background conditions of practitioners embedded in the commission for a longer duration. Thus, this study is practical those theorizing about how bureaucrats in African organizations can have autonomy and influence policy in the institution. Put differently, bureaucratic policy initiation needs to focus on the drafting of policy, speeches, and preparation of meetings and the substance and meeting that informs the content on those policies, speeches, and meetings. By focusing on meaning-making, this book contributes theoretically to the acquisition of agency by practitioners.

Policy Implications

This study has implications for policymakers who work on the substantive issue areas in this book. Below, I outline how peace and security, health, and private finance actors can benefit from the perspectives laid out in this book.

According to the African Union Peace and Security Architecture, RECs are meant to play an integral role in harmonizing continent-wide responses to governance issues. Although RECs are assumed to be under the domain of the broader African Union (AU), policymakers ought to consider the capacity of RECs, particularly their ability to leverage existing partnerships with stakeholders and use these partnerships for strategic reasons. Synergies between the AU and RECs need to be strengthened, and the processes laid out here offer a pathway toward supporting consensus and ownership over continental governance.

ECOWAS practitioners demonstrate through their actions and practices that there is an underlying idea of what regional governance in West Africa should be. Thus, in line with Article 16 of the AU Peace and Security Council (PSC) protocol, ECOWAS practitioners provide a model of coordination, close harmonization, and regular exchanges of information. The processes of convergence and agency outlined in this book help policymakers discern the intent and meaning behind these forms of engagement. Recognizing the agency of practitioners in ECOWAS also illuminates the methods and practices that can facilitate horizontal coordination and sustainability between RECs and between RECs and the AU. For example, ECOWAS's community levy and its strategic partnerships with RCSOs fill a sustainability gap present in other RECs and in some AU Commission departments. Policymakers could benefit from engaging with ECOWAS practitioners to leverage inclusivity as a resource mobilization strategy.

For health policymakers in West Africa, this study offers a pathway to engage with ECOWAS practitioners to deepen the understanding between ECOWAS and the relevant stakeholders. A key component of regional health and social policy is the need for inclusive coordination to sustain advances in regional health collaboration, balance the needs of health regulators across different scales of governance, and consider how an integrated approach to regional health governance can improve the capacity for vertical coordination between the region and national governments. As highlighted in Chapter 4, African Union Development Agency New Partnership for Africa's Development (AUDA-NEPAD) through the African Medicines Regulatory Harmonization program works with WAHO to develop a harmonized regional regulatory system for medical products and health technologies for ECOWAS countries. This kind of program provides a template that policymakers can use to strengthen regional health collaboration.

More importantly, policymakers can help ECOWAS practitioners develop more effective ways of implementing programs. As shown in Chapter 4, the WAHO's response to the Ebola outbreak in 2015 suffered from a lack of coordination between the region's technical, financial, and political partners. As policymakers within ECOWAS member states and beyond interface more with ECOWAS practitioners, they can also initiate and deepen the scope of learning and collaboration. This type of mutual exchange of expertise and understanding informs and builds upon practitioners' background knowledge, improving the proclivity for regional convergence.

The Future of Convergence and Agency

How will the region-building project in West Africa proceed? What makes the processes of convergence and agency endure? Although these processes of convergence and agency work to make the region-building project more durable, there are still challenges that persist in West Africa. While this book highlights the significant role of ECOWAS practitioners in regional health and regional finance, there remains a gap in the coverage of issue areas in ECOWAS outside of the scope of peace and security. Thus, the processes of convergence and agency offer an opportunity to explain ECOWAS's response to health outbreaks such as Ebola and COVID-19, particularly for those who consider the regional response limited in scope.

Though practitioners in peace and security, health, and finance all engage in processes of convergence and agency, they do so in common and varied ways. Practitioners across ECOWAS engage in the process of convergence by bringing together relevant stakeholders as part of an inclusive region-building process and are able to due to the space created by incremental shifts in the structure of ECOWAS. The conditions in which practitioners are able to participate in the process depend on the degree of institutionalization of practitioner autonomy in each area. For peace and security practitioners, the scope and depth of security actors and concerns in West Africa create the conditions for convergence processes to be more iterative and inclusive. As ECOWAS attempts to strengthen responses to those who break institutional rules (such as unconstitutional changes in government), the processes of convergence and the agency of practitioners will condition and determine what is in the realm of possibility in terms of responses.

The convergence process differs between peace and security practitioners and health practitioners, who are limited in their capacity to implement decisions. While there is variation in the processes of convergence, the practitioners are able to display their agency in similar ways, particularly by developing resource mobilization strategies and partnerships that allow practitioners to share the governance burden with other stakeholders. The convergence processes in regional financial governance vary from both peace and security and health, as the convergence does not necessarily occur in ECOWAS itself, but rather the processes of convergence give way for more private authority in West Africa. Institutional change occurs through national and regional policies and networks for practitioners to use to bring private financial actors to the region.

Taken together, these varied processes of convergence display how practitioners acquire and use their agency to impact the region-building project. Highlighting this agency is important in demonstrating how regionalism in West Africa operates on two different planes. The Heads of States occupy one plane, and another is occupied by the practitioners involved in pattered interactions with member states and non-state actors. These practitioners are responsible for making sense of and defining what futures are possible in the region-building project. The processes of convergence and agency advance our understanding of what is relevant to West African regional governance, why issues are framed as they are, and how ECOWAS as an institution can endure political, social, and economic volatility.

Index